TREE OF SALVATION

TREE OF SALVATION

Yggdrasil and the Cross in the North

G. Ronald Murphy, S.J.

OXFORD
UNIVERSITY PRESS

OXFORD
UNIVERSITY PRESS

Oxford University Press is a department of the University of Oxford.
It furthers the University's objective of excellence in research, scholarship,
and education by publishing worldwide.

Oxford New York
Auckland Cape Town Dar es Salaam Hong Kong Karachi
Kuala Lumpur Madrid Melbourne Mexico City Nairobi
New Delhi Shanghai Taipei Toronto

With offices in
Argentina Austria Brazil Chile Czech Republic France Greece
Guatemala Hungary Italy Japan Poland Portugal Singapore
South Korea Switzerland Thailand Turkey Ukraine Vietnam

Published in the United States of America by
Oxford University Press
198 Madison Avenue, New York, NY 10016

Library of Congress Cataloging-in-Publication Data
Murphy, G. Ronald, 1938–
Tree of salvation : Yggdrasil and the cross in the north / G. Ronald Murphy, S.J.
p. cm.
Includes bibliographical references and index.
ISBN 978–0–19–994861–1 (alk. paper) — ISBN 978–0–19–994862–8 (ebook)
1. Yggdrasil (Norse mythology) 2. Mythology, Norse. 3. Christianity and other
religions—Norse. I. Title.
BL870.Y44M87 2013
293'.13—dc23

2013003236

9780199948611

1 3 5 7 9 8 6 4 2

Printed in the United States of America on acid-free paper

To Georgetown University,
the lyre
between the caliper and the cross

each one heard them speaking in his own native language.
Acts: 2:6

Quidquid recipitur secundum modum recipientis recipitur.
Whatever is received, is received in accord
with the characteristics of the receiver.
Medieval scholastic axiom

CONTENTS

PART TWO
IN POETRY AND RUNES

PART THREE
IN YULETIDE CAROL AND EVERGREENS

ACKNOWLEDGMENTS

Looking back I can still feel the excitement of many years ago when I realized how great a role the evergreen tree and the stories of Yggdrasil seemed to have played in the conversion of the North. I even wrote an article on the subject for *America* magazine that appeared in its December 14, 1996, issue. Realizations, though, if they are going to be the subject of exploration for many years to see if they are borne out in real art and artifacts, require a fair amount of support. Interest and encouragement in the subject coming from fellow researchers and students and from a group like the Mythopoeic Society constituted a real incentive to continue. I received such interest and encouragement that it multiplied my own curiosity and thus this book has come to pass.

I would like in the first place to thank Jim Walsh, S.J. for his continual encouragement. It was there at the beginning and continued throughout this project. At the end, he proofread every page. There were others among my students who read sections as did Professor Jim Cathey, Marty Chase, S.J., and my research assistant, the tireless Andreas Grewenig, who made himself something of an expert on runes and Danish round churches. Gene Nolan, S.J. read the entire manuscript, as did Thomas Connelly, Jennifer Niedermeyer, and Judi Rocco. The conversations and remarks that followed these readings were a real intellectual prod to explore further. I would like to thank all, but these few will have to serve as symbols for those who deserve my thanks.

Teachers and interpreters of literature are often able to work in the library or study. This project required a lot more movement. On-site examination, and a lot of travel connected with it, has left me indebted to many people with whom I had only the briefest of meetings. I would like to thank the lovely Yorkshire lady who took me in out of the rain of the north of England, fed me lunch, and then went about the village of Middleton to find the key to the church so that I could see the famous Viking crosses housed there. There were many equally kind people in Norway on the old pilgrimage path from the fjord to the church to Urnes who were concerned that none of us flag in the summer heat.

When it comes to the acceptance and appreciation of the finished work there is no one I can thank more than Cynthia Read, executive editor at Oxford University Press. Once again, and now for the fifth time, I have experienced her deep understanding and appreciation of a manuscript dealing with religious subjects in contexts that are not always the most familiar. She is an unfailing guide and supporter for her authors, and simply a pleasure to work with. She even attends her authors' lectures. I was happily surprised to see her at one I gave at Fordham on the stave churches. I am also especially indebted to her able assistant, Charlotte Steinhardt, who did not even let Hurricane Sandy prevent her from attending to the nuts and bolts of preparing the manuscript for publication. Oxford's anonymous readers deserve real plaudits for their penetrating and detailed reviews. Their enthusiasm was a pleasure to read, and their suggestions for improvement were ones for which I am grateful. Almost everything suggested was included, especially those on transitions that were designed to make the book a smoother read.

In a book of this sort that sails out of range of the usual and familiar, illustrations are not just useful, they become indispensable. They serve, alongside all available images on the web, to make the subject matter immediately visible while reading. I am deeply indebted now once again to my friend and former student, Laurence Selim. After having worked on my previous fairy tale and holy grail volumes, she was instantly ready and willing to take on the task of illustrating, for example, tree burial in the pagan-Christian world of long ago. The reader may wonder why not just take advantage of the Wikipedia sites, or others, on the web. The problem is, of course, that those illustrations, though adequate for viewing on the computer screen, often do not have sufficient definition to make them suitable for printing in a book. Laurence made use of dozens of images to create each of her drawings, thus using their different perspectives to achieve higher clarity, and in the case, for example, of the eroded sculpture of the Descent from the Cross, even enhancing the definition for the reader.

For other images I have relied on Art Resource in New York, the former Zodiaque publishers in France, a free use image by Blad, and my own photographs. For the bracteates, we have consulted Hauck and Heizmann and the *Realexikon für deutsche Altertumskunde* as well as web illustrations. Coordinating all these photographs and drawings with text and production has been a formidable task. I would like therefore to thank Fordham University and its Modern Language Department and Medieval Studies Program for offering me the Loyola Chair, which enabled me to have the time to go about this very extensive and time-consuming labor.

Let me now thank the university that has provided me with the home base, the comfortable and encouraging environment for sharing research and delight in learning, without which none of this could or would have easily gone forward. Georgetown has been my academic and personal home since 1974. My deepest thanks and acknowledgment of indebtedness have to go to the Jesuit Community, to the German Department, and to the spirit of Georgetown. I feel grateful that I have always felt at home in Georgetown's classrooms and in writing and research, so well supported by friends, colleagues, and administrators, I scarcely know what to say. Perhaps the dedication page says it best.

TREE OF SALVATION

Chapter 1

Introduction: Yggdrasil and the Cross

When something comes home to you, something you have known and perhaps even understood for a long time, I call that a moment of realization. Knowledge can be held at a distance, but when it "comes home" to the person who knows it, it can have a startling or surprising effect that shows up in feelings and personal attitude. The concept is not new; Aristotle first described the phenomenon as "re-cognition," *ana-gnorisis,* when he was writing his laudatory critique of Sophocles' *Oedipus the King* in his *Poetics*. Sophocles has the plot of the play brilliantly lead up to the climactic moment of realization. Through a recollection of Oedipus's intellectual ability to answer the riddle of the sphinx on the nature of human beings, through investigation with interviewing and reasoning, the audience accompanies Oedipus's objective and analytical journey to find out who the guilty party is that is causing the plague. What he does not realize, of course, is that he is the one—he is looking for himself. When it comes home to him that he is the one responsible, and that he has been blindly looking for himself, he can only say, "O, O, O." For the Greek reader of the story, there is a further hint here that this tragic moment of realization has been the final purpose of the plot: the triple repetition of the "O" is a triple repetition of the last and final letter of the alphabet: Omega, Omega, Omega. He has reached the end of his search; what he is has "come home" to him.

Though realization can be tragic, or comic, as a level of knowing it is extremely important to religious devotion and art, since contemplative religion, and here, Christianity, thrives on its faith and beliefs, its images of salvation, "coming home" to the believer. In the following pages, we will take a journey through the world of the Anglo-Scandinavian-Germanic North, the world of Germanic culture, to see how the northern Europeans after having initially received Christianity in diverse ways, often somewhat suddenly through political-military means, gradually came to realize what they had accepted. They expressed this in the art objects that we will study, not by abjuring the religious feelings and basic images of their older Germanic faith, but by letting their more newly received Christianity "come home" to them, letting the new faith speak to them through the art and poetic imagery, the language, of their own Germanic religious culture.

In the Bible, it is often the Old Testament that is used to make the events of the New Testament come home to the early Jewish-Christian believer. The Exodus, for example, is used to encourage realization of the nature of Jesus's death; Jesus is called the "Lamb of God" in the New Testament to identify him as a temple atonement sacrifice, and as the fulfillment of the sacrificed lamb whose blood on the lintel and doorpost made the angel of death pass over the male children of Israel. The Crucifixion is alluded to and foreshadowed by the function of the bronze serpent that was hoisted on a pole in the desert to cure those fatally bitten by adders. Jesus's three days in the tomb is analogous to Jonah's three days in the whale. The difficulty, of course, is that these incidents from the Exodus and elsewhere in the Old Testament may help a Jewish Christian come to realize emotionally the meaning of things that they may not have seen before in the passion and death accounts. They are far less an emotional help, however, to those for whom the Old Testament does not contain familiar ancestral stories, and is thus not capable of being seen as a foreshadowing being fulfilled or coming true. Even as Old Testament stories become more familiar to northerners through instruction, the Old Testament is not quite their own historical, emotional, religious home. Learning its stories becomes more knowledge and, at least for a while, remains perhaps less than effective at eliciting a realization of the meaning of the cross, let us say, than also using their own myths of rescue.

The first author, poet, who addressed the problem in northern terms was the unknown author of the ninth-century *Heliand*.[1] He describes the Crucifixion as taking place on a tree; he implies that it was a hanging as well as being done with nails. Salvation by faith is explained as salvation by faithfulness, by loyalty, thus echoing the chieftain-thane structure of northern society. Mary is not just "full of grace"; she is someone for whom her Lord has great "fondness." "Blessed are the peacemakers" is given in a warrior society's terms as "Blessed are those who do not like to start fights or lawsuits." Amazingly, the entire Gospel story is what the author undertakes to turn into a realization text, a northern poem, one that will bring the message home to the Christian readers of the North. Did it do so? One little bit of evidence that it did have an influence is the copy of the *Heliand* that is in the British Library. When I held it in my hands I was surprised to see a little note written in Latin on the flyleaf, saying that the book belonged to Canute, king of England, Denmark,

1. For an excellent evaluation of the role of the *Heliand* in the transition, see Rachel Fulton, *From Judgment to Passion: Devotion to Christ and the Virgin Mary, 800–1200* (New York: Columbia University Press, 2002). In writing of Augustine's conversion through reading Scripture as described by Philip of Harvengt, she notes that conversion itself is "an act of interpretation, a translation from a clouded or alternative understanding of reality," pp. 378, 468.

Norway, and southern Sweden. Canute (also Knut, Cnut; born 985–995, died 1035) held his northern empire together by force, and also by encouraging cultural harmony. He was a Dane, and according to the inscription, was reading the *Heliand*, a Saxon gospel text, copied for him in East Anglia. It may be his spirit and that of Pope Gregory the Great (d. 604) that helped provide encouragement for several of the works you will see here.

The great cultural monuments treated in this volume, from the Jelling stone in Denmark to the stave churches in Norway, from *The Dream of the Rood* and the runes of the fuþark to the round churches on Bornholm and Viking crosses at Middleton in Yorkshire, and not forgetting the Christmas tree, are all indebted to the interweaving of cross and tree in the North. Their creation is an expression of northerners' realization of the rescuing function of Christ's cross in terms of the story of the evergreen Yggdrasil. To visit the sites and writings where evidence of this poetic rhyming of tree and cross can still be seen and felt is the journey of interpretation on which we shall embark in the following pages.

The myth of Yggdrasil is known to us mainly from two sources, the *Elder* or *Poetic Edda*, whose author is unknown, and the *Younger* or *Prose Edda*, of Snorri Sturluson. The *Elder Edda* is a collection of poems dating back to the ninth century. What we now possess of them is a copy which was written down in the thirteenth century, around 1275, in a book for the king of Norway, the *Codex Regius*. The *Younger* or *Prose Edda* was written in approximately 1220 by the Icelandic law-speaker and poet Snorri Sturluson (1179–1241). His compilation shows detailed awareness of the poems of the *Elder Edda* and Snorri both uses them[2] and expands beyond them. Both the *Elder* and the *Prose Edda* are invaluable for envisioning

2. Snorri must have been using an earlier version unknown to us as well as oral tradition.

the cosmos as seen by northerners before (and after) the coming of Christianity. Though Christianity came to the North around the year 1000, it is remarkable how the pagan stories and myths persisted so well that Snorri could write his compilation and expanded version of them over two hundred years later. By then, the stories and poems would have offered a certain pleasurable return to "the old days" for those who remembered them, hearer or reader, and it is not surprising that in the thirteenth century they were given the title *Edda*. *Edda* is the word in Old Norse for "great grandmother,"[3] a word that lends the figures and events of the tales, and the tales themselves, a certain family innocence and fairy-tale aura. "Great grandmother" gives them an acknowledged rootedness in the olden days, with tranquil assurance that the continuity of their ancestral pagan content is of no harm to the Christian present.

Yggdrasil, according to the *Edda,* is the great central tree that stands in the middle of the universe. It is the axis of the world, the world tree that holds up the skies, and the tree of life. It unites and separates the worlds of Asgard, high in the tree, where the gods dwell in their great halls, Middlegard where the human beings live in their smaller halls, and the damp and dark underground world of Hel, monstrous goddess of death. It is an extremely steady and yet dynamic model of the universe, a model that in its own way anticipates the more modern law of the conservation of matter and energy. Deer with heads thrown back and snakes among the roots and branches continuously feed on the tree, and yet, though it suffers, the tree always grows enough to balance the loss. The image of the tree in medieval times, as we will see in the following chapters, presents an interrelated concept of the world of above and below, of

3. See *Edda* in Rudolf Simek's *Dictionary of Northern Mythology* (Woodbridge, Suffolk: D. S. Brewer, 1993), p. 69.

the realm of plant and animal as mutually dependent and devouring, and of transformation of plant into animal, animal into plant. Modern images of Yggdrasil, by contrast, are more concerned with illustrating the relative spatial positions of the three levels, Asgard, Middlegard, and Hel, geographically as it were, than the more biological and dynamic interrelationship of plants and animals. They tend to see Yggdrasil mainly as the central pillar, like the Irminsul of the Saxons, that supports the three worlds (actually nine, the three can be subdivided) and the sky, and which provides a safe structure with boundaries—which indeed it does—as it holds the inhabited worlds and the sky. Yet it is alive.

On top of the tree sits an eagle with a hawk on its brow; the eagle beats its wings and produces the winds of the world. Underneath the tree at the roots of Yggdrasil and devouring the corpses of the dead is the horrible and frightening figure of the Nidhogg, the dragonlike snake that continually attempts to eat the roots of the tree of life and feeds on corpses—seeing to the annihilation of the dead. A squirrel runs up and down the tree carrying insults between the eagle and the snake, but they stay in their separate realms. Yggdrasil supports the worlds and reaches beyond Asgard to hold up the sky and all the stars; thus one can see the shapes of some of its invisible branches at night by observing the stars and following their outlines in the constellations.

During the long winter nights one can look up at the northern circumpolar sky and see the Big Dipper slowly making its way around the pole star.[4] The cosmic world tree is called Ygg-drasil, meaning "the awesome one's horse, or mount." The awesome one is

4. Douglas Simms, writing about the Saxon Irminsul, has suggested that early Scandinavian high-seat pillars, set up within a hall with a "divine nail" at their top, symbolized the point of connection between the world-pillar and the night sky as it revolved around Polaris. See his "The Sun and the Saxon *Irminsûl*" in *Vox Germanica, A Festschridt in Honor of James C. Cathey* (Tempe: University of Arizona Press, 2012), esp. pp. 78–80.

Woden (or Odin), and Ursa Major is still known as "Odin's Wagon" in Scandinavia, and you can see him slowly riding around the pole star at night. Another explanation is also given for calling the world tree Yggdrasil "the awesome one's horse." Odin "rode the gallows" when he hanged himself on Yggdrasil, making the tree "the horse he rode" when he made the ultimate sacrifice of himself to himself, to learn the secret of seeing the future. He seized the runes or talking sticks (presumably from the Norns, though this is not said), the cut and inscribed twigs of Yggdrasil, on which these three mysterious women[5] who know the past, present, and future, wrote the twenty-four secret letters by which the future could be divined. Later the runes came to be used by men, a gift of Woden. This myth will be important for reading the fuþark.

The other road of communication, aside from the squirrel and the rune twigs, is the rainbow bridge which is often visible in daylight soon after a rainfall. It runs from the base of Yggdrasil up to the world of the gods, Asgard. After nightfall, it can be seen twinkling brightly in the darkness of the sky as the great frosty arch of the Milky Way. It is thus, I believe, that there are two words for the bridge between the worlds. It is called both the bifrost, as the Milky Way, and also bilrost, as the rainbow.[6] In many religions, the

5. Their three names, Wurd, Verdandi, and Skuld, indicate fate or the inexorable flow of time; literally the names mean "happened," "is happening," and "shall [happen]."

6. This is my interpretation of the possible origin of the need for two words for the bridge: to suit two concepts of it. One word indicated glimpses of the bridge seen as the rainbow during the daytime, the other indicated the bridge's shimmering appearance as the Milky Way at night. *Bil·röst* has been explained as composed of *bil* "place, time, weak spot" and *röst*, "current, way, road" or even "red or multi-colored." *Bif·röst* is also generally divided as *bif* "trembling, shaking, [shimmering?];" and *röst*, "way, road." My second suggestion is that *bifröst* could also have been understood as *bi·fröst*, or perhaps originally *bif·fröst*, making the word then be the [shimmering] "frosty" [way, road], fitting for a nighttime appearance of the bridge as the white, icy road across the dark sky, the Milky Way. For discussion, see "Bilröst" in John Lindow, *Norse Mythology, A Guide to the Gods and Heroes, Rituals and Beliefs* (Oxford/New York: Oxford University Press, 2001), pp. 80–81.

Milky Way is the ghostly road that souls take on their last journey. In Germanic religion it is used by the gods to come to the holy place at the base of Yggdrasil for their assemblies, and also to take their last journey to fight their final and fatal enemies at Ragnarok.

The base of the great tree is very important and very holy, as Snorri reminds us. It is there that the gods assemble, but it is also there that the pooled water and mud from the well of time is splashed on Yggdrasil's trunk and roots by the three Norns, thereby sustaining the great tree in existence. This description of the holiest place, the tree trunk with a font of water at its base, is one that will have an effect on marking the interior of churches as holy places. It will suggest a placement for the baptismal font in proximity to the central support of the church, and it will suggest something of the holiness of the congregation that comes together in the sacred spot at the foot of the tree where gods were once thought to assemble. This is a key to understanding the Ruthwell cross, the stave churches (in which Snorri may have worshiped during his trips to Norway), and the round churches of Bornholm.

Yggdrasil has three great roots extending out from the tree. No one knows where they come from or in what they are stabilized. Thus the type of tree that Yggdrasil is, is unknowable, though it is always simply referred to as an ash, the *askr Yggdrasills.* This ash is an evergreen standing over the wellspring of Wurd or fate, and since the ash tree is deciduous and not evergreen in the north, this again means that the Awesome One's evergreen "ash" has a mysterious, untraceable nature, sustained in life by the water poured on it by the three "weird sisters" of the flow of time. Medieval artists in the North depict Yggdrasil on occasion as a vinelike tree full of hungry living beings, and on occasion as a stolid evergreen spruce, the highest of trees. Both images seem fully justified by the Eddas.

In addition to supporting, feeding, providing a sacred place for meeting, and establishing continuity and communication among the beings of the world, perhaps the most famous of the many functions of Yggdrasil is to provide protection, especially at the mythic time of the end of the world, Ragnarok, the twilight of the gods, the fate of Woden, Thor, and Frey.

Compared to the Mediterranean world, it comes as a surprise that Germanic culture does not conceive of the gods as immortals. Despite the many equivalencies found between Germanic and Greco-Roman gods, for example, Woden = Mercury, Tiw = Mars, Freja = Venus, and so forth, one equivalency was never supposed, that the gods of the North are immortal as are the gods of the South. Instead, the radical concept of the end of the world found in the Eddas is simply that it is the end of the gods. Naturally the world is also destroyed at Ragnarok, but it will reemerge, and some gods and their gaming board will survive; the main gods, however, will never be seen again. Most important for us, however, is the question of what the story of Ragnarok says about the fate of human beings?

The first sign of the coming of the end will be three continuous winters in a row with no pause for summer in between. Then the calamity will begin. The age of the axe and the sword will come with kin fighting kin, humans slaughtering one another in an age of immorality, all bonds of kinship losing their strength, animals battling and devouring each other, as the enemies of the gods begin to assemble for the final battle. Heimdal will blow his horn to warn the gods to assemble, as the sun and moon are devoured by the great wolf Skoll and fierce dog Garm that break loose from their chains. The Midgard serpent will break loose from his confinement to the ocean that encircles the land and will thrash his way onto the shore, causing tidal waves of terrifying destruction and spewing poison as he goes. The fire giants led by Surt will come from the south bringing the "harm of branches," forest fires, flinging firebrands in every direction setting off the incineration of the whole world. The tree Yggdrasil will begin to tremble and shake. As the fire giants march up the rainbow, the Milky Way, the bridge will crack and break under their weight. The stars will fall from heaven and the volcanoes will erupt more fire as the gods lose all control. After a terrible struggle, Woden will be swallowed by the wolf Fenrir, whose horrible jaws are so big they stretch from the top to the bottom of the world. Thor will kill the attacking Midgard serpent, Jormungand, with his hammer, but the dying serpent will so spray him with venom that he will take only nine steps backward and fall dead. Frey will do battle with the fire giant Surt and they will both lie dead at the end of it. The ghostly armies of the dead from Hel will clash on the Vigrid plain with Woden's warriors marching from Valhalla and annihilate each other. The earth begins to sink into sea.

At this point comes the most amazing part of the story. The trembling Yggdrasil, seeing and feeling the destruction of the whole world which the tree supports and protects, will open to the last man and woman, or boy and girl, Lif and Lifthrasir, to admit them and provide protection for them throughout the end of the world. Even while Ragnarok is proceeding outside, and the tree is trembling itself, its wood will provide safety and life for Lif and Lifthrasir, and will give them the dew of the morning to keep them alive.

> Lif and Lifthrasir, and they will hide
> in Hodmimir's wood;
> they will have the morning dew for food;
> from them the generations will spring. (*Vafthrudnir's Sayings*)[7]

7. *The Poetic Edda*, Carolyne Larrington, trans. (Oxford/New York: Oxford University Press, 1996), p. 47. The "wood," Hodmimir's Holt, is a kenning for Yggdrasil understood as a tree, though some others prefer to see it as a grove.

And the return to Yggdrasil is really a mythical return. Both man and woman are made from tree trunks (Snorri's Edda), or from driftwood and vine (Elder Edda), found on the seashore by Woden; thus the Edda depict a deep relationship in nature across time between the human race and the wood of Yggdrasil. It is no wonder then that the tree Yggdrasil is trembling for the fate of the world, but opens up to hide its two relatives, man and woman, and to protect them from the rage and death of Ragnarok.[8] The Christmas carols we will examine later still contain echoes of this distant vision of mankind in the songs of the "holly and the ivy" during the winter cold.

At the end of Ragnarok, a new earth will emerge from the sea, there will be the daughter of the old sun to shine in the sky, the stars will return, and there will be a new moon. The earth will come up from the ocean, eternally green as the prophetess predicts a new and happy world of new life:

> She [the prophetess] sees, coming up a second time,
> Earth from the ocean, eternally green;
> the waterfall plunges, an eagle soars over it,
> hunting fish on the mountain.
> . . . .
> Without sowing the fields will grow,
> all ills will be healed, Baldr will come back. (*Voluspa*)[9]

Instead of chopping down the symbolic ash or spruce trees, in view of this legend and prophesy, it is very clear that Christianity

8. There may be a similarity here to an event in *Hrolfs saga*, ch. 28, at the moment when King Adils finds himself under attack by Hrolf in his hall. "When Kind Adils saw what they were doing, he saved himself by running to the tree that stood in the hall. The tree was hollow, and so he used his magic and sorcery to escape from the hall." *The Saga of King Hrolf Kraki*, Jesse L. Byock, trans. (London: Penguin, 1998), p. 62.

9. *The Poetic Edda*, Larrington, trans., p. 12.

could, and eventually did, see this story as a kind of parallel to Old and New Testament stories. It is the wood of the tree that provides salvation for Life and Life-eager by giving them shelter from the fire at the end of all things, and by providing them with the drink that comes from its own branches. One can almost hear the words from the Last Supper. The promise of a new life after the end is also something that cannot be far away from Christian thought. The trembling tree, having feelings of fear for the world and concern for the human beings in its branches, is a remarkable testimonial in itself that the world is not completely unconcerned, but the heart of creation is somehow aware, and aware of human status and existence. Why would one feel it necessary to get rid of such a beautiful belief? Not only was it not entirely done away with, but it comes to beautiful reexpression in the burial crosses in Yorkshire in which are embodied the amazing realization the cross embodies the protection promised by Yggdrasil—the dead are safely hidden and protected inside the new wood of Yggdrasil, Christ's cross.

And what of the Nidhogg that the devours the corpses of the dead and threatens the roots of Yggdrasil itself, and against which Yggdrasil can do nothing? I journeyed to Yorkshire to see what the artist of the Middleton crosses had realized, if anything, about that, and saw that the answer, given in traditional Germanic terms of binding Garm, Fenrir, and Loki, was there. One thing that the cross could do that its predecessor Yggdrasil could not was stop the mouth of the dragon-snake by providing for the resurrection of the dead.

The chapters ahead will explore the hermeneutic relationship between the tree and the cross in the North by going roughly backward in time. In Part I, we begin by looking at the twelfth- and thirteenth-century stave churches of Norway and the meaning of their wooden structure and design, and then the contemporaneous round churches on Bornholm in Denmark with their central pillar.

Next we look at the tenth-century burial crosses in Yorkshire and the meaning of what they depict, there being no Christ on the cross. In Part II, we change genres and enter the world of the written word and carved runes. *The Dream of the Rood* and the Ruthwell cross bring us back to the eighth century as we read the function of runes carved on the cross—talking staves enabling speech on the part of the rood. The following chapter suggests that the sequence of the runes in the fourth century fuþark might be a possible mnemonic based on the Yggdrasil myth itself, influenced by Christianity. Evidence for this is given in a close examination and interpretation of the fascinating iconography of the migration-period c-type bracteates, clearly related to the myth of Woden, the runes, and the tree. Finally, in Part III, we transfer to the genre of tree-related ritual, considering the ancient pre-Christian and Christian role of the evergreen in winter. We go back to the oldest, continuous ritual use of the evergreens—still to be found in the context of the winter solstice, the birth of Christ, and the changing of the year: the Yule wreath and the Christmas tree.

As prelude, let us consider briefly an example from Denmark.

There is a monumental rune stone in Denmark erected by Harald (Harold) Bluetooth in the tenth century, in approximately 960–970, in honor of his parents and himself that can serve as our introduction.[10] It is a truly monumental, gigantic granite boulder of some ten tons, standing approximately seven feet in height, tilted slightly, and shaped like a naturally rounded three-sided pyramid, carved on all three sides. It stands between two barrows, or burial mounds, that had been erected for Harold's father, Gorm the Old, and Gorm's wife

10. For historical context, see Elsa Roesdahl, *Viking Age Denmark* (London: British Museum Publications, Ltd., 1982), 159–93. Her volume also contains a good illustration of the griffin on Harald's rune stone, p.192. The color in it has not been restored, but the background is helpfully blackened, making the intertwined image of snake and griffin quite clear. There is no attempt at interpretation of the images, however, in her text.

Thyra, next to a church whose wooden predecessor was on the same site. The site is a good one for considering the time of transition from the old faith to the new. When the barrow of Gorm the Old was excavated, it was found to have a burial chamber, but no body was in it. The quality and position of the artifacts in the chamber suggested that the corpse had been removed, rather than the burial chamber plundered. The body was later discovered to have been reinterred under the floor of the church next to the monumental boulder, which is itself at the centerpoint between the two barrows; the body had gone from the old style burial to that of that of the new religion's in hope for eternal life. Harald, Gorm's son, had removed his father's body from the wooden chamber under the barrow and reburied it under the wooden cross in the early wooden stave church.

The stone, which was originally painted in brilliant colors, has an inscription that runs along all three sides, with the majority of it filling one side [a] and then it continues with the last phrases under the images on the other two sides. The inscription is carved in runes and reads, [side one:] "King Harald ordered this monument to be made in memory of his father Gorm and his mother Thyre. That Harald won for himself all Denmark; [at the bottom of side two:] and Norway; [at the bottom of side three:] and made the Danes Christian." Side two has an anticipatory mythic depiction of a lethal battle between a griffin and a giant serpent that has entwined its coils around the griffin's neck, midsection, and tail. Griffins were fabulous animals of two natures, eagle and lion, lord of the skies and the earth, and so were often used in the middle ages as a symbol for Christ.[11] Snakes were their enemies. Side three has a most

11. For a fuller discussion of the griffin, see Louis Charbonneau-Lassay, *The Bestiary of Christ*, D. M. Dooling, trans. (London/New York: Penguin [Parabola, Arkana]), 1991, pp. 397–409. The Jelling griffin has the eagle's head, the talons, and the erect ears along with the lion's body that identifies it as a griffin. In some cases only the female griffin had wings, and the Jelling sculpture does not.

remarkable depiction, in accord with the words of the inscription appropriately carved under it, "and made the Danes Christian:" (Figure 1.1) the Crucifixion. This most unusual depiction of Christ crucified as being fully entwined with plant tendrils and being held bound by them echoes the adjacent image of the griffin and its battle with death.[12] The Crucifixion as carved on side three is truly a Danish image done as if the artist realized in local Germanic mythology what the cross of the crucifixion and death meant. One could almost add to the inscription "and made the Danes Christian," the comment "and made the Crucifixion Danish."

Because there is an analogous poetic concept behind the great twelfth century apse mosaic at San Clemente in Rome, it might now be useful to compare the Roman with the Germanic images.

Life emerging from death, the time of spring following that of winter, new green shoots coming forth from the old gray branch, Lazarus being summoned forth from his tomb, all this lies at the heart of the Christian mystery. To depict this unexpected paradox, Christian artists and storytellers have often suggested that the wood of the cross on which Christ experienced death was really from the tree of life in the Garden of Eden story. The early twelfth century mosaic filling the apse of the church of San Clemente in Rome depicts the motif we are about to examine at Jelling in its Mediterranean form: the cross is a shoot emerging from an acanthus bush. The tendrils and leaves of the acanthus fill the whole apse, enclosing in shoots and branches all the living creatures of the world, while twelve doves (for the twelve apostles) settle on the vertical and horizontal limbs of the cross on which Christ is bleeding and dying.

12. For recent discussion of the association of Christ with Odin on the Jelling stone, see Henning Kure, "Hanging on the World Tree: Man and Cosmos Is Old Norse Mythic Poetry," in *Old Norse Religion in Long-term Perspectives: Origins, Changes, and Interactions*, Anders Andren et al., eds. (Lund: Nordic Academic Press, 2007).

Several items in the depiction tie this vast image to a realization of the identity of the acanthus cross as given in Old Testament prophesy. The four rivers of Eden mentioned in Genesis (2:10–14) as flowing out of the Garden to water the earth—the Pishon, the Gihon, the Tigris, and the Euphrates—in the apsidal mosaic are flowing out from the base of the acanthus that is the source of the cross. The Psalmist's deer[13] with heads down are drinking from the waters of life that flow from the cross. Interestingly, the cross itself is not totally identified with the acanthus. The artist has placed a large Greco-Roman acanthus at the base of the cross, but the cross is depicted as quite distinct from the plant. The cross is given a very dark almost black color and is geometrically perfect with arms at a 90 degree angle from the upright. The acanthus leaves and tendrils, even the crown of thorns, twist in luxuriant swirls and circles; they encircle, but they are no part of the angular cross nor do they at any point touch, let alone confine, the Crucified. The acanthus is identified with the tree of life from Eden; the cross is treated as an offshoot, but also as quite clearly distinct.

The mosaic of San Clemente reminds the observer of all that happened in the Garden of Eden story, especially the fall of Adam and Eve that brought with it the punishment of death. Christ is shown on the cross as accepting that punishment for mankind, while the snake is curled at the base of the acanthus. The death of Christ on the cross is a redressing of the mistake, turning the tree of the knowledge of good and evil by means of his cross into the tree of life[14] with the birds in its branches and

13. Psalm 42:1: "As the deer pants for streams of water,/so my soul pants for you, O God."

14. The poetic-homiletic conflation of the two trees, the tree of knowledge of good and evil and the tree of life, in Christ, has a long tradition, from Augustine to Alger of Liège, Hugh of St. Victor, and St. Bonaventure. See Ann W. Astell, *Eating Beauty, The Eucharist and the Spiritual Arts of the Middle Ages* (Ithaca and London: Cornell University Press, 2006), pp. 27–40.

the four streams of Paradise emerging at its foot to give life to the thirsty deer. In the Middle East, the tree of life and the tree of the knowledge of good and evil were seen as possibly olive trees and date palms, but to make it come home to the Romans the poet of the mosaic preferred to use the local, and classical, Greco-Roman symbol for luxuriant life, the acanthus, and to associate it with the cross.

In the North, with a different mythology and a different story of a tree of rescue, how could one depict such a realization of the achievement of the Crucifixion so that it could be equally familiar and moving to an Anglo-Scandinavian with his own myth of a tree of life? The acanthus is not biblical but it has deep roots in Greco-Roman iconography, and for the Roman Christian poet of San Clemente deeply aware of his own tradition it seemed appropriate. In the North, we are indebted to the poets who realized what the Crucifixion meant using their own iconographic and mythic tradition. For the artist of Jelling "bringing it home" would be to see the cross not as a luxuriant classical bush, nor the tree of Eden's waters, but as the living tree that holds up the universe, the tree that rises alongside the well of time, the evergreen Yggdrasil.

To do so the artist uses a foreshadowing from the world of classical myth, the griffin with the entwining serpent, to show that the death of Christ on the cross was a titanic struggle of a being with two natures, with the strength of a lion and the heavenly sight of the eagle, against the suffocating coils of death. There are no nails in the scene. Christ is not held to the cross by being nailed, he is held to the tree Yggdrasil by having come to live in it, in Middlegard, by having accepted a lifetime among human beings in the tree of life, and thus he accepted the measurings of the three Norns, including death.

Figure 1.1. The crucifixion as depicted on the great memorial stone at the royal site of Jelling in Denmark. The memorial was erected by King Harold Bluetooth to commemorate his parents and his own achievements, especially the conversion of the Danes to Christianity. The stone is dated to 965 AD, and ends with the king's statement, under the Crucifixion, that he "made the Danes Christian." The stone was originally brightly colored with the entwining vine possibly green but the paint has worn away. Werner Forman/Art Resource, New York.

Most surprising for a Roman visitor would be that the Danish Crucifixion scene has no cross.[15] One can hear the observations that the figure must be the god Balder (despite the cruciform halo), or that it is simply "barbarous." Both observations have been made. Yet to a medieval theologian the depiction would smack of the necessary connection of the Incarnation to passion and death. If God

15. Also true in the Crucifixion panel on the Gosforth cross. The whole of the Yggdrasil shaft is the cross at Gosforth. A separate cross within the panel would be redundant and detract from the composite identity of the vertical shaft as Yggdrasil/cross.

becomes an actual human being, then certain things will have to follow; the wood of the cross will stem from the wood of the manger. To be born, to be or become finite, is to accept the need to die. And thus in opposition to the mosaic at San Clemente where the cross is quite distinct from the acanthus plant from which it springs, at Jelling it is the vines and branches of the tree of life itself, Yggdrasil, that bind Christ to dying. There is no need for anything as artificial as nails, nor is there any need for a separate and distinct wooden cross. Henning Kure, seeing a possible analog to Woden's hanging in the tree in the *Havamal*, noted,

> Hanging on the world tree is a representation of being in connection with the spiritual spheres—or maybe even of becoming that connection. . . . We may see this concept at work on the great rune stone of Jelling. Its portrait of Christ hanging on the cross is well known. On closer inspection, however, we may note that there is actually no cross. Instead, he seems entangled in branches, a clear visual of connecting with the tree.[16]

Christ himself is present in the tree wearing a white tunic with his arms fully spread out in the crucified position, his feet straight down as if he were indeed on the cross, which he is. The vines twist and turn around him, holding his arms, his midsection, and his feet securely in position, bound just as is the griffin next to him. The entire rock face is covered with the vines that end in knots and leaves, joining the knotted vines and tendrils that cover the edges of the entire boulder on all three sides. Christ is entwined in Yggdrasil. He is like the tree Yggdrasil itself which will one day itself tremble in

16. "Hanging in the world tree," in *Old Norse Religion in Long-Term Perspectives, Origins, Changes, and Interactions*, Anders Andrén et al., eds. (Lund: Nordic Academic Press. 2006), pp. 69–70.

fear of the end, and like Woden who hanged himself in the branches of Yggdrasil to learn the runes of the ultimate future. Like all who are born he is subject to the passage of time, the Norns, and to what they weave and carve on the staves, on the twigs cut from the tree of life, including the cutting of the thread of life. In less northern language: "He was crucified, died, and was buried."

And yet the sculptor did not quite leave it there; he realized something more and it can be seen in his clothing the Crucified in a white tunic. Christ is wearing the white robe that recalls what he was often named in the North, *hvite krist,* the White Christ. Christ is associated with the tree Yggdrasil that is supporting him bound in mortal life, but also with the white robes of the Resurrection and the shimmering light of the bifrost, the white and ghostly road that leads up to heaven. The author of the *Heliand* (c. 830) seems to have had a similar realization when he described the Christ's rising from the dead, going from starlight to heaven road.

> The warriors sat on top of the grave on their watch during the dark starlit night. They waited under their shields until bright day came to mankind all over Middlegard, bringing light to people. It was not long then until: there was the spirit coming, by God's power, the holy breath, going under the hard stone to the corpse. . . . the many bolts on the doors of Hel were unlocked; the road from this world up to heaven was built (*uuas. . . . te himile uueg giuuaraht fan thesaro uueroldi*)! Brilliantly radiating, Gods's Peace-Child rose up![17] [5765–5776]

17. *The Heliand, the Saxon Gospel,* G. Ronald Murphy, S.J., trans. (New York/Oxford: Oxford University Press, 1992), pp. 190–1. Of course, one cannot be sure if the *Heliand* poem was of any influence on the sculptor of the Jelling stone, but the cultural moments are similar.

The god Thor who was attacked by the Midgard serpent, as is the two-natured griffin on the monument, took nine steps backward and died, never to be revived. The White Christ, with his divine and human natures, was able to accept death in the world tree when the fated time came, and was able to die and to rise in radiance from death, frustrating the serpent, and creating a light-bridge, a bifrost that extended far beyond anything imagined by the notion of Woden's Asgard and Valhalla.

Harald Bluetooth was the grandfather of Canute the Great, mentioned above as owner of the British copy of the *Heliand*. Harald was the Christian son proud of his pagan father, Gorm the Old, and of his mother Thyra. The monumental stone he had erected to them shows his appreciation of them both.[18] Harald had turned not only the Danes Christian but also himself. The artist of the monument must have admired Harald's loyal effort to rebury his pagan parents inside the church in a final gesture to see that they attain Christian heaven. The sculptor's artistic insight was that he realized a way to express the graciousness of Harald's loyalty to his parents' religious spirit: the parents' Yggdrasil and the son's cross are one. *Utraque unum.* This notion is a key to the interpretation and appreciation of several of the most fascinating works of art of the Middle Ages.

18. And perhaps also a political need as well. See the political reconstruction of events as suggested by Birgit Sawyer in the excursus "The Tug-of-War over Turf," in her *The Viking-Age Rune-Stones* (Oxford/New York: Oxford University Press, 2000), pp. 158–66.

PART I

IN WOOD AND STONE

Chapter 2

Yggdrasil and the Stave Church[1]

The *Heliand,* with appropriate alliteration, calls the cross on Calvary a *bôm an berege,* a "tree on a mountain," an appropriate designation with which to begin this study of the relationship between a tree and a church. The stave church has been the subject of much research and appreciation, the majority of which has focused on the stave church's remarkable and long-lasting wooden construction. The debate continues to this day on how much of the stave church's style is an import from the continental South, the basilica translated into wood; how much is from the Celtic, Anglo-Saxon church of the British Isles; and how much is from the North. The focus of this paper is on the North, the role of Germanic religion and myth in the style, with the aim of attempting to interpret the overall meaning of the design of the stave church.

Peter Anker and Paul Hamlyn's wide-ranging study of the question accepts Andreas Bugge's rejection of the view that the portals of the stave church, for example, normally had no specific Christian content and that the portals were purely decorative in intention. They also look positively on his suggestion that the portal ornamentation might be allegorical pagan iconography of Christian ideas. They add, however, "In fact this question has never been subject

1. This chapter appeared in an earlier form in a tribute to Professor James E. Cathey in *Vox Germanica* (Tempe: University of Arizona Press, 2012).

to serious scholarly investigation, and Bugge never did discuss the matter in detail."[2] To which one could add: unfortunately. This I would like to address in some small way.

It is my theory that a good model for attempting an approach to understanding the religious meaning and style of the stave church is the *Heliand*. In the *Heliand,* the story of salvation by Christ is told in the language and poetry of the north, the poet imagining cultural equivalencies in order to transform the gospel story into an epic, often while retaining the original as well. One of my favorite examples is the scene of the Annunciation, where the term "grace" is both translated and also repeated literally, a poetic technique of creating rhyming concepts through analogy or parallelism. Instead of "Hail Mary, *full of grace,*" the angel Gabriel is made to speak two languages: first he says to Mary, "Your Lord is very fond of you," thus touchingly interpreting grace as God's fondness, and then he adds literally from the Latin text as well, "woman full of grace."[3] Even the fate of Judas is given in both languages. Judas hangs himself, as in the Bible, but the *Heliand* author also adds, "cruel things started going into his body, horrible little creatures, Satan wrapped himself tightly around his heart."[4] A sad echo of the fate of the Gunnar who betrayed Siegfried and who for his disloyalty was thrown into a snake pit.

Perhaps more important for us here is the analogy in the *Heliand* drawn between the cross and the tree, the cross as *bom an berege,* a tree on a mountain.[5] In the *Heliand's* crucifixion scene, Mary under

2. Peter Anker and Paul Hamlyn, *The Art of Scandinavia,* vol. 1 (London, New York: Hamlyn, 1970), p. 416.
3. *The Heliand, The Saxon Gospel,* G. Ronald Murphy, S.J., trans. and comment. (New York, Oxford: Oxford University Press, 1992), p. 12.
4. *Heliand,* p. 152.
5. See especially Songs 65 and 66: the cross as "a new gallows, the wooden tree," "hewn with battleaxes," "out of a hardwood tree," Pilate's inscription is "wisely cut into the wood." Christ hangs from a "criminal tree." *The Heliand, The Saxon Gospel,* G. Ronald Murphy, S.J., trans. and comment., pp. 182–88.

Figure 2.1. The Borgund stave church seen from the southwest. The path leading down to the left ends at the western entrance. On the roofs and walls wooden shingles are everywhere, giving protection from rain and snow. The lower gables end in crosses, but on the upper gables are prominent serpents. The low stone wall encloses the church's graveyard. Author's photograph.

the cross is described as standing under the tree, Christ is described both as being nailed to the cross and also as hanging by a rope from the tree, and when he is stabbed with the lance, the size and power of the lance and its thrust are made so impressive that an echo of Woden's stabbing on the tree Yggdrasil[6] is hard to miss.

I would like to suggest that this particular style of creative (and retentive) transformation of the gospel story into Germanic story images and events is the poetic key to the transformation of the church building into the stave church. The church is the holy place, the site of the protective presence of Christ, and above all the place of the act

6. The name Yggdrasil alludes to this event. Ygg: "Awesome One" [Odin] + drasil: "horse, mount, steed." The tree acting as a gallows for his death is thus the "horse" that he "rode" in dying. "Odin's horse" is a kenning for that mythic evergreen ash, just as "whale road" is for the sea.

of salvation in the mystery of the Mass and the sacraments. How does one express "holy place," "site of rescue from annihilation," in the Nordic world? Does Nordic myth have any appropriate analogy—even one that may have already been influenced by Christian story?[7] Snorri Sturluson (1179–1241) gives the familiar answer in the *Gylfaginning* that the chief holy place is at the tree Yggdrasil:

> Then spoke Gangleri: "Where is the chief center or holy place of the gods?"
> High replied: "It is at the ash Yggdrasil. There the gods hold their courts each day."
> Then spoke Gangleri: "What is there to tell about that place?"
> Then said Just-as-High: "The ash is of all trees the biggest and best. Its branches spread out over all the world and extend across the sky."[8]

In the *Poetic (Elder) Edda,* the seeress adds in the *Voluspa* that this unusual tree, which is called an ash, is evergreen.

> I know that an ash-tree stands called Yggdrasill,
> a high tree, soaked with shining loam;
> from there come the dews which fall in the valley,
> ever green, it stands over the well of fate[9] (*stendr æ of grœnn Urþar brunni*).[10]

7. Because pagan beliefs and practices have been transmitted through Christian writers, some believe that the descriptions of paganism stand under some Christian influence. This seems plausible to me, particularly in the case of the spear thrust in the hanging of Woden/Odin on Yggdrasil, and as an offering of himself to himself, a formula in the Byzantine liturgy.
8. Snorri Sturluson, *Edda*, Anthony Faulkes, trans. (London, Rutland, VT.: Everyman/Orion, 1995), p. 17.
9. *The Poetic Edda*, Carolyne Larrington, trans. (Oxford: Oxford University Press, 1999), p. 6.
10. *The Elder or Poetic Edda, Part 1—The Mythological Poems* (London: The Viking Club, 1908), p. 282.

The ecclesiastical holy place in the South is the basilica. The basilica shape so common and appropriate in Mediterranean Christianity suggests an analogy of the church to the Roman magistrate's court, a long, horizontally extended, rectangular building embodying the law-administering authority of the king, the *basileus,* with the magistrate seated separately at the far end in an apse as judge to protect the innocent and punish the guilty. The stave church retains some of the basilica in often having a choir and apse; the sanctuary, separated from the main body; and the nave. But there is also an additional transformation of "holy place" and "site of rescue" into the tree language of the North as well, with a shorter, more square nave and powerful staves to facilitate a vertical extension (Figure 2.1). The Christian language of salvation in the North seems to have been aware of the Germanic story of ultimate salvation, one not based on a story tradition of the protective power of law and authority but based on a story tradition long known and familiar in Norse and Germanic society. The protection and salvation of the human race by rescuing the last boy and girl, Lif and Lifthrasir, at the end of time would be accomplished by the Tree of Universal Life, Yggdrasil, by hiding and protecting them throughout the calamity and by feeding them with the tree's dew. My suggestion is that the stave church is a Christian Yggdrasil, based on the poetic insight that there is an appropriate analogue in the North by which to express the concept of the place of salvation: it is to translate salvation as the inner space of Yggdrasil, the holy wooden place of protection at doomsday, and that at the heart of the evergreen tree's space is Christ on his wooden tree, the cross.

I will try to substantiate this interpretation by looking at three aspects of the stave church: (1) the shape, (2) the portals and door, and (3) the interior; and by interpreting several of the allusions and symbols found in the poetic form of stave churches, principally in that of Borgund in connection with shape, Urnes in connection with

Figure 2.2. Interior view of the east end of the Borgund stave church, showing the wooden staves or pillars, and the fished arches made of knees. Up above are the x-shaped struts (the St. Andrew's crosses) which serve to bind the stave structure together. They are carved with patterns of stylized leaves on branches. The nave is somewhat small but comfortable, as is the sanctuary, but what the church may lack in grand floor space it makes up for in height. Author's photograph.

the portal, and Uvdal from the point of view of the interior. Finally, we will take a look at the famous Swedish tapestry from Skog, which actually shows a functioning medieval stave church. I visited many of these churches to get a firsthand feel for them, and also because, though all have some of the aspects, no one of them has all the tree aspects to the same degree. And I wanted to know what it was like to walk into them. There were some surprises.

First, Peter Anker's definition of stave church:

> The Norwegian word *stav,*[11] which means pole, applies to the corner posts and columns which are essential for upholding the

11. The English word stave, as in barrel stave, is related; as is the word staff, a pole held in the hand.

> entire structure, and for joining the fundamental chassis to the upper braces. The *stav*, or pole is the most obvious characteristic of these buildings. . . . the stave church can be defined as a wooden building constructed with timber balks and posts linked to frames, the frames being put together into three-dimensional, cubic structures, with the covering materials – the wall planks – fitted into the frames where convenient. In addition to this, the stave system implies a number of advanced technical solutions – bracing, joining shoring, etc., which are necessary for its final architectural expression. [He goes on to say what a stave building is not: a building with horizontal logs like a log cabin.][12]

This is a good technical definition of the wooden construction of the churches. It is significant that no attempt is made at defining the church part of the "building." From this the reader can see an indication that the greatest fascination has been with the amazing survival of 800-year-old wooden buildings, and with their truly fascinating manner of construction. The interpretation of their meaning has been neglected in comparison. The building of stave churches is dated from about the middle to late eleventh century, with the twenty-eight that are still in existence dating from about 1130 until 1350—about the time of the black plague. There is evidence of earlier structures on the sites of several churches whose current building dates to the twelfth century. In one case, at Urnes, excavators found a coin under a posthole dating from the time of Harald Hardrada, who died in 1066 AD.[13] Since the official date for

12. Peter Anker, *The Art of Scandinavia*, vol. 1 (London: Hamlyn, 1970), p. 377–78.
13. This is the Viking king Harald Sigurdsson who invaded northern England in 1066 to press a claim for the throne and who fell at the battle of Stamford Bridge outside York. The place and timing of his invasion in the North was a help to William the Conqueror, whose almost simultaneous invasion, also in claim of the throne, was in the distant South. The resultant Anglo-Saxon forced marches to the South may have resulted in the Normans facing a less than fresh army at the battle of Hastings.

Norway's conversion to Christianity is 1000, these unique churches and their predecessors stem from early stages of conversion and Christian-Germanic accommodation, and continued to be built for almost 300 years.

I am sure there is some question as to whether the Anglo-Saxon missionaries from the British Isles would have felt at home using pre-Christian, pagan ideas of a holy site for a Christian church in Norway. In this connection it is useful to recall the famous letter of Pope Gregory the Great (590–604) to the Abbot Mellitus to establish policy for the conversion of the Anglo-Saxons themselves. He says he has been thinking about the issue of the conversion of the English for a long time, then:

> Tell Augustine [St. Augustine of Canterbury] that he should by no means destroy the temples of the gods but rather the idols within them. For, if those temples are well built, they should be converted from the worship of demons to the service of the true God. [*Nam, si fana eadem bene constructa sunt, necesse est, ut a cultu daemonum in obsequio veri Dei debeant commutari*]. Thus, seeing that their places of worship are not destroyed, the people will banish error from their hearts and come to places familiar and dear to them in acknowledgment and worship of the true God. Further, since it has been their custom to slaughter oxen in sacrifice, they should receive some solemnity in exchange. Let them therefore, on the day of the dedication of their churches. . . . build themselves huts around their one-time temples and celebrate the occasion with religious feasting . . . if they are not deprived of all exterior joys, they will more easily taste the interior ones. For, surely it is impossible to efface all at once everything from their strong minds, just as when one wishes to reach the top

> of a mountain, he must climb by stages and step by step, not by leaps and bounds. . . .[14]

Gregory's approach to the conversion of the North was that of moderation and cultural accommodation. The word he used above to express his idea that the pagan temples, *fana*, should not be destroyed but be converted—*com-mutari* [lit. "co-" + "changed"]—is far closer to a notion of fair or appropriate exchange, in the respectful style of the *Heliand*, than to that of the tree-felling St. Boniface and the Irminsul destruction of Charlemagne. Though the idols must go, the temples, if well-built and based on beautiful tales, well, that is another story, a tradition long practiced in Rome itself.

Few wooden structures are as well-built as the stave churches, as time has shown. Because of their closeness to the end of the Viking period, and because of the use of several ship-building techniques, the Norwegian stave churches have been associated with the Vikings. There is evidence for this (Figure 2.2). There are truly remarkable support arches in the church, which, despite appearing to be perfect arches, are actually composed of two "knees" joined by being "fished" together. Both knees and fishing are techniques used by the Vikings in wooden boat building. Knees are naturally curved wood taken from the part of the tree where the roots turn on an angle to become the tree trunk. Knees are much stronger than wood sawn into a curve. Fishing is a technique of joining two pieces of wood together on an angle, a bit similar to that used in botanical grafting, in which, for example, one piece of a mast is joined to another. The arches in the stave churches are so well made, the two halves so well joined, or fished, by a diagonal juncture at the center of the arch, that at first glance the arch does not look like two knees

14. http://www. fordham.edu/; also in Bede, *Historia Ecclesiastica* I, 30; and in *Patrologia Latina* 77: 1215–16.

but like one sawn arch. However, this having been said, the joining of the main staves themselves to one another by inlet bracing and high sills, with tongue-and-groove joining of the vertical wall planks to one another and to the corner staves, indicates to me that landsmen, professional carpenters, were also at work. Sailors will know of the Norwegian lapstrake or clinker-built[15] technique of planking the hulls of Viking ships—no trace exists of that method of joining and waterproofing that I have seen in the stave churches, only the tongue-and-groove method with vertical planks, not strakes. It seems that those Vikings who stayed at home and built temples and halls passed on their brilliant techniques every bit as well as those who sailed the sea did.

"Norway spruce (*Picea abies*) and Scots pine (*Pinus sylvestris*) provided most of the construction timber" for the stave churches, notes a lumber expert[16] speaking of the church at Borgund, and that is not surprising since a drive through southern and central Norway shows that the conifers, rising exceptionally straight and as high as giant lodgepole pines, seem like an unending carpet for the country. It seems at first, however, that ash would be the preferred wood for a stave church that is an allusion to Yggdrasil. However, there must have been some considerations. The first is poetic: the northern ash is deciduous; the leaves fall with the coming of winter. The pine as candidate for Yggdrasil, Tree of Life, has the distinct advantage, comforting in the long winter, of displaying that it is alive by remaining ever green. There may also have been two

15. A Viking shipbuilding technique in which the horizontal strakes, planks, of the hull are made to overlap each other, not to join edge to edge. The Oseberg ship and the two others in the Viking Ship Museum in Oslo are examples. The hull itself is thus such a strong, integral unit that it does not need the extensive internal bracing that a carvel-built [edge to edge planking] boat must have.
16. Aljos Farjon in his *A Natural History of Conifers* (Portland, OR: Timber Press, 2008), p. 208.

more practical considerations, abundance and flexibility. The evergreen conifer is extremely abundant, straight-trunked, resinous, and strong in Norway, ideal for building. I do not believe that the ash is as abundant, as resinous, or as straight and strong. Ash-wood in short lengths combines toughness with a high degree of flexibility that makes ash ideal wood for oars and hand weapons associated with Odin such as spear shafts and axe handles, as well as gallows for hanging.[17] This might make ash less than suitable for tall church construction where flexibility might not be thought of as a virtue by the congregation underneath the high roof. The mysterious ever-green tree was the most suitable wood for creating a wooden building to parallel Yggdrasil, the tree that is, in any case, so holy and mysterious and its roots so deep that no one really knows where they come from, keeping its profound and enduring nature beyond human ken.

The abundant pine tree provided not only the wood for the church, but also the pine tar or pitch to act as a sealant with which to paint and waterproof it, and, I would like to suggest, to be the very model for the shape of the stave church. The matter and form of the edifice, in good Aristotelian style, are in harmony. No attempt is made to twist the roof to resemble the ash. A surprise for me was that a tarred stave church can actually be smelled as you approach it—it has a distinct smoky pine odor. The church betrays in many ways the tree from which it is made.

THE SHAPE

The resemblance of the roof structure to the cascading branches of an evergreen is unmistakable as one approaches the church at

17. And in the United States, of course, for baseball bats.

Borgund. This church is so well preserved, and has been so little altered over the intervening eight centuries to our time, that it has become the most accepted archetype of the stave church and is most worth studying. Since we are dealing with the perception of form, it is worth contemplating the shape that the roof structure gives the church, that of an evergreen. As one approaches the church from a distance it looks like a dark pine tree in a forest, with the familiar conical, Christmas tree shape as it stands on the lower part of what becomes a steep, wooded slope. With other trees around it, it looks different from them by its darkness, caused by the coating of pine tar.[18] As you get closer it looms up higher and higher with the ascending gables and roofs creating the illusion of layers of pine branches. Finally, as one stands at the western entrance and looks up, the pine tree effect is enhanced by looking at seven roofs, one on top of the other. In ascending order, the lowest and broadest roof covers the walkway or ambulatory that surrounds the whole church; it has a shingled gable over the entrance. This is topped by a second roof, slightly smaller in diameter, also with gables parallel to the lower roof, which covers the side aisles inside the wall staves. A bit higher there is another quite small gabled roof above the west window. A fourth roof covers the nave of the church, and a fifth peaked roof covers the small bell tower or turret that rides saddleback on the nave roof below it. Above the bell turret there are two more roof structures, functionally unnecessary, but contributing mightily to a vertical succession of diminishing roofs and gables, two small peaks with a terminal spire that give the clear impression of the peak of a pine tree. This is an impression that is curiously and effectively strengthened by the almost dominating presence of shingles that

18. The current approach lane to the Borgund church is from the north; thus the church appears dark for two reasons: the sun is on the opposite side of the building, casting the north side in shadow, and the tar coating lasts much longer on the side not exposed to sunlight.

completely cover every roof, the external round staves, and the outer walls of the church except for the sides of the ambulatory and of the bell turret. Anders Bugge noticed this as well when he wrote:

> The wooden shingles which covered the six roofs [he is most likely not counting the small roof over the west window as a seventh] and most of the side walls beneath them, provide a surface effect similar in appearance to a pine cone. In the same way the tall, slender pyramid-shaped building reminds us of the fir. . . . The many roofs of the church, decreasing in size with height, are a striking parallel to the clustered branches which narrow towards the top of the tree.[19]

And I might add, the flat, lozenge shape and regularity of the shingles with their sawn off tips immediately suggest the cones of the Norway spruce. Unfortunately, Bugge did not use this very accurate observation to go any further toward an interpretation of its significance in signaling the identity to the stave church.

But we are neglecting the most obvious and most striking element of all (Figure 2.3). On the upper roofs of the church there are large serpent heads projecting from the gables, heads erect and alert, tongues extended, jaws partly open, ready to bite. Then, placed parallel to the snakes on the two lower roofs, are wooden crosses above the peaks of the gables. The combination is the most striking feature of the roof profile—striking, but like a striking contradiction. What religious evergreen could there be that is associated with snakes? And how could it be associated with Christianity? Though many think that the snake heads and the crosses are there to repel evil spirits from a holy building, I think they serve another purpose

19. Anders Bugge, *Norwegian Stave Churches* (Oslo: Dreyers Forlag, 1953), p. 13.

Figure 2.3. A view of the Borgund church from the west southwest, showing the tiers of roofs as they decrease in size as the eye goes upward, suggesting the shape of a pine or spruce tree. The bell tower rides saddleback on the third roof and has sides that are carved with openwork to let the bells's sound pass. The next two roofs constructed above the bell tower seem to have no structural function except that of giving to the building the shape and profile of an evergreen tree. Author's photograph.

that is more important. They serve to give a holy identification to the building.

> Three roots there grow in three directions
> under the ash of Yggdrasil;

> Hel lives under one, under the second the frost-giants,
> the third, humankind. . . .
> More serpents lie under the ash of Yggdrasil
> than any fool can imagine:
> Goin and Moin, they are Grafvitner's sons,
> Grabak and Grafvollud,
> Ofnir and Svafnir I think for ever will bite on the tree's branches
> [*meiþs kwistu*].
> The ash of Yggdrasil suffers agony
> more than men will know:
> a deer bites it from above, and it decays at the sides,
> and the Nidhogg [serpent] rends it beneath.[20] (*Grimnismal*)

There is not only the Nidhogg serpent devouring corpses and the roots of the tree beneath, there are also countless snakes in the tree itself, in the branches. In other words, the *Grimnismal*'s depiction shows that snakes should be in and on the gables of the stave church if it is a representation of the suffering and holy tree Yggdrasil.

In the rhyming-concept style of the *Heliand*, the roof shape and snake ornaments address the observer of the church in Germanic, the cross ornaments address the observer in Christian; both saying in alternate languages: *this site is holy*; you are near the place of the Norns, near the well of life and threat of doom and death, you are standing under the tree; realize that here you are near Calvary and standing under the cross. This is the place and here is the mysterious wood where the ancestral, predictive *Edda* stories tell of the hanging sacrifice, the offering of Odin to himself, god to god. This is the sacred wood where it came to pass, where God the Son hung, offering himself as a sacrifice to God the Father "once, and for all." In the

20. Larrington, pp. 56–57.

Poetic Edda Odin speaks about his death on this tree whose origin and nature no one knows:

> I know that I hung on a windy[21] tree
> nine long nights,
> wounded with a spear, dedicated to Odin,
> myself to myself,[22]
> on that tree of which no man knows
> from where its roots run.[23] (*Havamal*)

Parallels were present. In the Gospel stories of Jesus's death, Jesus also complains that he is thirsty and bemoans his abandonment by the Father, and at the end commends his spirit into the Father's hands. There is also the spear. "When the soldiers came to Jesus and found that he was already dead, they did not break his legs. Instead one of the soldiers pierced his side with a spear, bringing a sudden flow of blood and water."[24] Alluding to the death of Odin by the shape of a Christian church building—the church in Hegge, at the top of a stave, actually has a depiction of Odin's head as he is being strangled by the rope—makes the Germanic religion serve as a recontextualization for the Christian mystery. (See Figure 2.4.) In the New Testament, events from the Old Testament are used to explain and prophesy, to contextualize, those of the New. Christ's death is an "Exodus," he is the new "Passover Lamb." He will bring a new and better "Exodus": not from Egypt to Palestine

21. "Windy" helps identify the tree as the one on top of which the great eagle fans his wings, creating the winds, Yggdrasil.
22. This line seems to echo the formula of sacrifice used of Christ in the Eastern (Byzantine) Eucharist. Addressing God the Father the priest says: "we offer to you yours of your own." This formula could have reached the North perhaps by way of the Rus or possibly by way of Christian Vikings returning from mercenary service for Constantinople.
23. Larrington, 34.
24. Jn 19: 33–34.

but from earth to heaven. In the stave churches, as in the *Heliand*, local religious tradition is made instead to serve this purpose. Christ's death was, like Odin's, a death on a Tree. It is therefore a mysterious death—whose roots no one knows. Stabbed with the spear, Odin in his death reached down and seized the powerful runes and gave them and their magic to mankind; Christ, stabbed with the spear, poured out his blood and water, giving them, his sacred runes, to mankind in baptism and Holy Communion. To use the Germanic religion as an interpretive context for the Crucifixion only adds another layer of meaning to the richness which comes from using the Hebrew Torah and prophets for this purpose.

THE PORTALS

The western portals of the great stone cathedrals in continental Europe depict the last judgment. Christ is enthroned in the place of judgment above, the scales are under him weighing the souls of the just and the unjust, and the angels are leading the good to paradise on his right and the devils are busy leading the bad off to the jaws of hell. The scene above the main door to the cathedral urges the Christian to hurry inside so as to be one of those on the right. In the North this is doomsday, Ragnarok. After the succession of three mighty winters without spring or summer, the unmitigated violence among animals, the elements of heat and cold, and human beings will begin:

> Brother will fight brother and be his slayer,
> brother and sister will violate the bond of kinship;
> hard it is in the world, there is much adultery,
> axe-age, sword-age, shields are cleft asunder,
> wind-age [winter], wolf-age, before the world plunges headlong;

Figure 2.4. The head of the hanging god, Woden, blind in one eye with tongue hanging out from the rope. This head is carved at the top of a stave in the Hegge church. Photograph by John Erling Blad.

no man will spare another.

. . . .

Heimdall blows loudly, his horn is in the air.

. . . .

Yggdrasil shudders, the tree standing upright,

the ancient tree groans and the giant is loose;
all are terrified on the roads to hell,
before Surt's kin [flames] swallows it up.
. . . .
Surt comes from the south with the harm of branches[25]
. . . .
Men tread the road to hell and the sky splits apart.
[Oden is swallowed by the cosmic wolf; Thor by the earth-encircling serpent]
Then the powerful, mighty one, he who rules over everything,
will come from above, to the judgment place of the gods.[26]
There comes the dark dragon flying,
the shining serpent, up from the Dark-of-moon hills;
Nidhogg flies over the plain, in his wings
he carries corpses. . . ."[27] (*Voluspa*)

The portals of the stave churches depict doomsday as conspecific violence even with the winged serpent Nidhogg present. Many of the portals have winged serpents at the top of the arch, blowing an evil wind across the nine worlds. In a few cases the violent judgment of evil takes place. In the Hylestad portal, now a part of the antiquities collection of the university museum in Oslo, Siegfried is shown stabbing the dragon from below and then running his sword through the heart of the treacherous Regin so that blood is spurting from his chest, back, and mouth. Just above on the left side of the same portal, the traitorous Gunnar is in the snake pit. The great majority of the magnificently carved portals, however, depict writhing

25. "The harm of branches" is a kenning for fire, forest fire. Surt is the leader of the fire-giants.
26. These two stanzas sound like a Christian insertion, saying that God will come to the sacred place of the tree Yggdrasil, the well, and the Norns. This would fit with the stave church.
27. Excerpted from the *The Poetic Edda*, Larrington, pp. 10–13.

snakes, dragons, griffins, and even bears[28] intertwined in violent conflict with one another, twisting and turning in and out of the entangling vines, leaves, and branches. In some cases the snake and dragon tails become vegetation, their tails turning into lilies, letting the observer know that the carver was aware that he was telling a story: a violent myth of life at the end as mortal conflict with the mutual eating, biting, and destroying of one another.

Perhaps the most famous of these portals, and seemingly the oldest, is at Urnes in Sognefjord. I took the journey to the little church on the hill side through some of the most beautiful scenery in the world. Norway's fjords, especially the Sognefjord, are breathtaking. As I crossed the ice-cold, blue-green water, I looked up at the walls of stone on both sides, and up and down the immense stretch of mountain on both sides, awestruck at the beauty of the canyon-like walls and the snow covered peaks in the distance. To get to Urnes, it is necessary to take a second ferry across a smaller fjord, since there is no real roadway to the stave church except by circling around the entire length of the fjord. When you reach the landing on the far side, you realize there is now a hillside to climb in the heat, and the locals told us that pilgrims had made this route uncomplaining even in their times, and probably in medieval times as well. The view from the church, as with many of the stave churches, is spectacular. One of the reasons that the churches truly have to make an impression is to counterbalance the overpowering sight of the mountains and the fjord, visible right from their front door.

And the doorway makes an impression (Figure 2.5). Using the language of the *Elder Edda,* the visitor is told how important and holy is the door he or she is about to open. The door is simply

28. Bears fighting, with one attempting to bite the tongue out of the mouth of the other are at the top of the right door jamb at the western portal of the stave church in Heddal in Telemark.

Figure 2.5. The magnificent portal now placed on the north side of the church at Urnes in Norway. It was probably the principal entryway on the western end of the 1070 AD church, symbolically powerful but perhaps a bit narrow for practical use. The entrance may have had to be widened, and these staves removed, but they were saved by being used on the north wall. A deer with head thrown back is on the left side; a snake emitting a fleur de-lis on the right. The artist has deliberately created a combination of life forms—deer, snake, branch, and vine—so interwoven by elongated, coiling forms, that the eye does not make a ready distinction between the intertwined living things of the tree of life—with the significant exception of the deer with his head thrown back to feed on the tree and being bitten by a serpent. Author's photograph.

surrounded with whorls of writhing snakes and vines. The tangle is so perfectly executed in a welter of animal elongation and plant reduction to vines, that it is difficult to identify where a head begins or where a tail finally ends, if at all, or to trace what seems like a joint to a neck or a leg or a vine. The main point seems to be the intertwinedness itself of all living things, animal or vegetable, in one huge tangle. On the right hand side, about one-third of the way from the bottom a serpent is even emitting a fleur-de-lis from its mouth. So well done is this doorway that it and its imitators are referred to by art historians as exemplifying the Urnes style.

Now as one looks at the left side of the doorway there is one animal standing on four legs that is simply startling in the clarity of its depiction. It has been called a lion and explained as the Lion of Judah (Christ) fighting with evil. I think that such an interpretation makes the mistake of using an inappropriately biblical explanation when the artist by his very Viking-like pictorial style, as well as his tangle of animal and plants, tells you he is here using a Germanic one.

If you look at the animal you can see that he is eating at the vine or branch which in turn is a serpent biting at him in the neck (Figure 2.6). Look at the animal's head and you can see two small horns protruding—that animal is a young male deer, a hart. Now it becomes clear, it is not the Old Testament that is giving the context here for the meaning of the portal; this is an allusion to the *Elder Edda* and its description of Yggdrasil as the suffering tree with many serpents forever biting on its twigs and branches, as those twigs and branches are also being devoured by a hart.[29] The tradition of the single deer may also come from a previous stanza in the *Grimnismal* where the hart is named: "Eikthyrnir [Oak-thorn] is the hart's name, who stands on the Father of Hosts' hall and grazes Laerad's [kenning for Yggdrasil] branches; and from his horns liquid drips into Hvergelmir [seething cauldron], from thence all waters have their flowing."[30] In any case, the carver has simply drawn the inference

29. In the stanza preceding the serpent stanza, it is also mentioned that there are four deer gnawing at the branches. This would give the artist the choice of using one or four deer to identify the doorway as Yggdrasil.

30. Larrington, p. 55 and n., p. 270.

Figure 2.6. Close up of the deer eating at the tree of the vine-branch-snake as it in turn bites him in the neck. Author's photograph.

that the branches/snakes would defend themselves as well as they could by biting back at the deer. All of this serves quite deliberately to identify the portal as Yggdrasil. But if this is so of the doorway, what of the door?

The artist has associated the door with the portal by the sparest and most ingenious of means. At the top of the door a section of vine-serpents overhangs the door itself, not just a feat of carving, but it also makes the door belong to the life tangle on both sides of it. Then, he has changed the door from a flat, nondescript surface to a surface carrying low relief whorls of vine and animal. The low relief serves both to make the door different and yet to keep it closely associated with the door jambs' vines and serpents. If the door jambs depict the branches and the deer then the door between them must be the tree trunk: the tree trunk of Yggdrasil being gnawed at by the deer with the short horns. The two hinges can just be seen on the right side; the larger is about one-fifth of the way from the bottom. To enter the door of the Urnes stave church is to enter Yggdrasil.

That this theme or insight may have been commonly understood can be seen not just in Norway, but also on the famous door of the stone church at Roglösa in Sweden. (See Figure 2.7.) This door is interpreted often as being a saint's legend or as a pastoral hunting scene above with a Garden of Eden or last judgment scene below.[31] In my opinion the door could just as easily be seen as representing the "last days" in Germanic form. Such a reading of the wrought iron on the door accounts for more of the figures present. Examining the bottom left we see the first clue: a large serpent is slithering toward a tree, his eye on its roots. This must be the Nidhogg. (If it were Satan, by tradition it would be higher up in the tree and have the customary apple in its mouth, Lucifer having no known taste for roots.) The tree whose roots are about to be gnawed is unusual in that all its branches, which are writhing rather than straight, end in serpents' heads. To the right of the tree a naked monster with flames for hair and claws on its feet is stabbing (and melting!) a woman with a fire stick—the monster Surt, the black, fire-giant leader from the South. To his right the observer sees a winged soldier being attacked by a two-headed dragon that is biting his shield with one mouth while the mouth at the other end is spitting out poison over the warrior's head. This could be Thor, with his Viking pigtail, fighting the Midgard serpent which killed him with its spewed poison. Thor seems conflated somewhat with Michael, the fighter of Lucifer, by having wings, but not Michael's iconic spear. He appears to be holding a weapon in his hand but it is small, perhaps a hammer.

31. Aron Andersson and Paul Hamlyn, *The Art of Scandinavia*, vol. 2 (London, New York: Hamlyn, 1970), illus., p. 235; interp., p. 348.

Figure 2.7. The door of the main portal of the church in Roglösa, Sweden. Normally seen as a hunting scene above with Adam and Eve below, I believe it is announcing Ragnarok. Above Heimdal blows his horn, summoning the gods for the final battle. A wolf and a dog are loose next to him, Fenrir and Garm, and a deer chews on the framework with antlers tilted back. The descending eagle may be Woden himself, talons out to attack Fenrir. Down below, at the bottom a snake approaches the roots of the tree, as the fire giant, Surt, is spewing fire and burning and melting a goddess, while Thor fights a poison spewing serpent with a head at each end. A goddess, Freya, holds up a tree leaf; it is an ash, and behind her the great pattern of an ash leaf rises to the top of the door. She is pointing to the church door handle, the way to safety inside the ash of Yggdrasil. Photograph by Zodiaque.

Changing to the top panel in the arch we see someone blowing a long horn, as well he should be, if the double-headed Midgard serpent is attacking and Surt and the fire-giants are advancing. If this is Heimdall blowing his warning horn for the gods, then this depiction is of Ragnarok, the Day of Doom, with the unleashing of the wolf Fenrir, and Garm, guard dog of hel. To the right in the arch the deer, a hart, is tearing bark off the tree and unhurriedly eating—another evidence that Yggdrasil is not far away. The eagle descending may well be Woden himself in disguise, claws extended to attack. In the left lower panel there are two representations of trees—mistakenly, I believe, said to be the two main trees from the Garden of Eden—the lower one, just mentioned, with roots and serpent, and another one above, with no roots. Between the two, a female figure is pushing away the serpent head of one of the branches, and her other hand is holding up a branch, a sign of plenty. This would suggest that she is Freya, goddess of happiness, prosperous crops, and plenty. The branch she is holding up is of the same shape as the large "tree" in the upper left corner—it is simply an expanded version of the leaf pattern in her hand which she is showing the person about to enter the door. Like her branch, it has six leaves arranged in parallel and one at the tip—the leaf pattern of the ash: Yggdrasil. She is holding up the identity of the door in her hand, the ash, and serving her appropriate function as identifying the way to survival and prosperity.

The whole wrought iron outer framework of the composition contains, despite its almost geometric regularity, little fiddlehead plant shoots that emerge irregularly out of the frame onto the composition it edges and contains. The door thus has two representations of the tree of life in the lower panel, with serpents and with the ash leaves, as well as the iron door framework itself, which is subtly revealed as the organic frame for all that happens: it is Yggdrasil, and the time is Ragnarok. Time to open the Yggdrasil's door, let the little bells on the door-ring chime, and enter into the saving tree (which just happens to be the church).

Looking at the eleventh century south (side) portal of the Vågå church, Bugge comments:

> A large dragon has coiled its body down the semi-column on the right side of the doorway, and driven its fangs into the threshold. . . . Lions and dragons wind their necks about the round arch, where, supported by columns, it seems to terminate a free standing arcade in the middle of the welter of animals. Around the left half-column grows a tree with cunningly interlaced branches and leaves, possibly the Tree of Life, *Yggdrasil,* surrounded by the clamor of the world.[32]

There is more here, I think, than the clamor of the world, especially since the carving is on a church entrance. Bugge however did recognize the presence of Yggdrasil, and goes on to suggest more when he writes of the Hoprekstad portal:

> Here we meet the classical stave church portal, fully developed in a doomsday picture on a par with the west front of contemporary Continental cathedrals. It is a native Norwegian translation of the latter. By means of a powerful "kenning", as in a scaldic poem, the destruction of the powers of Hell is shown in a self-destructive *Ragnarok,* outside the door of the very shrine they had come to destroy.[33]

I fully agree with the connections made regarding Yggdrasil and Ragnarok but believe Bugge missed the implication for the nature of a doorway and the church. As I mentioned before in connection with the roofline, Bugge's instincts point in the right direction; I

32. Bugge, p. 19.
33. Bugge, p. 24.

suggest only that he should have gone an important step further. It is not enough to consider the jambs of the doorway with their vines and violence. If this doorway depicts the branches and brutality of Ragnarok so famously described in *Voluspa*, then what is the door itself, positioned between the portal carvings, but the tree trunk, entrance into Yggdrasil itself? The church door provides an entrance into the suffering tree that is the rescue and salvation from the chaos and apocalyptic violence of the end of the world.

> *Odin said*:
> Much I have travelled, much have I tried out,
> much have I tested the Powers;
> which among men will live when the famous
> Mighty Winter [fimbulvetr] comes among men?
> Vafthrudnir answered:
> Life and Lifthrasir, and they will hide
> in Hoddmimir's wood,
> they will have the morning dew for food;
> from them the generations will spring.[34]

But the only way to escape the annihilating violence in the real world is to open the church door and go in. To open the wooden door is to repeat in reality the story of Lif and Lifthrasir in the only

34. Larrington, p. 47 and n. p. 269: "From the connection between Mimir and Yggdrasil noted in the *Seeress's Prophesy* [*Voluspa*] it is possible that Hoddmimir [Rememberer of the Treasure/Place] is another name for Mimir [Rememberer], and that the two survivors hide in Yggdrasil." I would add that the repeated connection between the source of dew and the tree Yggdrasil under several names is also evidence. It seems that this unexplained figure, Hoddmimir, was the personification of "the memory of the hoard," the sacred place where the treasure: the Tree of Life, the well of fate *([w]urd)*, and the passing of time (the Norns) were to be found. The word translated here as "wood" is *holt*. It can mean trees, wood, woods, and as here used in connection with Mimir, it functions as a familiar kenning for the wood, whether imagined as single tree or grove, that Hoddmimir minds, i.e., Yggdrasil.

way it can be repeated and actually done, the only way that exists by which to enter the mythic tree trunk. Once inside, the rescued will be fed the real dew that falls from the Christ crucified on the tree and given the real runes of the scriptures and Communion.

THE INTERIOR

Standing inside the church, or standing inside the wood, you see a complete absence of the snakes and violence of the portal. Looking up to the front the first thing that meets your eye in the gentle darkness and candlelight is the crucified on his cross, immediately over the arches between the main staves supporting the eastern end of the church.[35] The crucifix fits in perfectly with the x-shaped supports, the St. Andrew's crosses, that tie the main staves to one another. The rood screen is the statement that the entry into heaven is through the cross. It is impossible to say what poets might have imagined that Lif and Lifthrasir would have seen once they entered the protection of Yggdrasil, but the crucifix is an image of security and suffering, an invitation to the visitor to come in further. The x-cross stave supports on both sides of the crucifix are carved, at Borgund and at many of the churches, with vegetation motifs so that they extend the notion of leaves and branches inward and provide an appropriate accompaniment to the cross. The image of Christ, after crossing the 12 inch high sill at the door, seems to reassure that Ragnarok and violence have been left outside. The fact

35. The crucifix has not survived in all the stave churches and in some has unfortunately been displaced to the left of center to balance an oversize pulpit. The ones that have survived, as at Urnes with Mary and St. John on either side of Christ, are quite large in proportion to the eastern end of the church. Done with feeling, they focus the attention on the sanctuary and altar.

that weapons had to be left outside in the ambulatory may have contributed as well to the atmosphere of peace and sanctuary pervading the interior. At the church in Torpo and at the church once in Ål, now at the Oldsaksammling of the university museum in Oslo, there are enormous baldachins at the eastern end of the church with life-size images of Christ. Smiling at Torpo, head bowed in death at Ål, each is a masterpiece of personal presence. This is what, or who, lies at the heart of the tree that shelters life, even when life is in extremis. In the university museum it is worth looking up and studying the whole baldachin from the crucifixion at one end to the last supper at the other. As you look up and go through the days of creation and scenes from Christ's life, there is one depiction that may startle you, Christ carrying his cross on the way to Calvary (Figure 2.8). The cross he has shouldered is not made of the usual planed boards—instead, outsized stumps are visible all over it from sawn off branches—it is a tree, and the color of the tree he is carrying is revealed at the crucifixion scene—it is green. The old Vikings need not fear that their deepest hope, expressed in the idea of an ultimately protective evergreen tree, will have been disappointed, Christ will carry it.

There is a cross in the Oldsaksammling of the university museum that goes even further in relating the cross to Yggdrasil. This cross is depicted with live and growing vegetation (Figure 2.9). It no longer has a corpus on it, perhaps appropriately, for down at the bottom of the cross, where one would normally expect to see the skull and bones of Adam being touched by the blood of Christ, there is a scene even more appropriate, the harrowing of hell. In the medieval Roman South this scene would be borrowed more from Virgil, with Christ, descended into hell, standing at the door of the underworld's dark cave, leading the souls of the dead through the rectangular doorway out into the light. The Oslo cross has the same scene

Figure 2.8. Detail from the baldachin of the church at Ål. Christ carrying his cross. The exaggerated length of the stumps of sawn off branches serves to show the cross to be a tree. The artist even painted the stumps of the branches red to make them more obvious and perhaps also to bring the tree's weeping from its wounds into association with the wounding and suffering of Christ. As in the *Dream of the Rood,* the painting associates Yggdrasil with the cross. From the Oldsaksammling of the University Museum in Oslo. Author's photograph.

but the depiction is northern. Hell's gate is not a cave but the mouth of an enormous snake, whose jaws are being forced open by Christ, whose feet are standing on the monster's lower jaw in a posture reminiscent of Vidar's tearing open of the jaws of the wolf Fenrir (Figure 2.10). One by one the dead are climbing out of the serpent's enormous mouth, amazement in their eyes, with Christ reaching in to take one by the hand who is stumbling on his way out. The artist sees Christ's cross as an Yggdrasil that can save far more than the last two of the living, Lif and Lifthrasir. Christ's tree is depicted as an Yggdrasil that can rescue those whose corpses have been devoured by the Nidhogg—the harrowing of hell is the Nidhogg being forced to release the dead.

Figure 2.9. Large stave church cross ornamented with vegetation from the Oldsaksammling of the University Museum in Oslo. Author's photograph.

Walking into the church at Uvdal, I had another surprise. At Borgund, one is surrounded by tall staves, pillars that could easily suggest a grove in the candlelight, as if the interior were like being in a forest. The same is true in the sanctuary at Kaupanger, but at Uvdal and at Nore the visitor in medieval times would have seen no pews and no ceiling and not too many staves, for, there in the middle of the room is a huge pillar rising up to support all the spreading branches

Figure 2.10. The harrowing of hell painted at the bottom of the cross. Christ has his feet on the lower jaw and his hands on the upper jaw of the serpent, the position of Vidar when he killed the wolf Fenrir. With his other hand he is helping one of the astonished and wide-eyed dead to rise from the jaws of the devourer of the corpses of the dead, the Nidhogg. Oldsaksammling, University Museum, Oslo. Author's photograph.

of rafters, braces and roof wood, turret and shingles (Figure 2.11). There the congregation would have been grouped around the shelter and strength of the tree trunk, another way to depict the entrance into the sheltering protection of the true Yggdrasil. Looking up at the staves and the carved heads at their tops, whether just a pun on "capital, *caput*, head," or embodiments of the ancestors, or the spirits of the felled trees, or even representations of the masked god, Odin, or even of the carvers of the capitals, it seems a good way to express that "we're all in this together," regardless of the time in which we lived. So the writer of the old Norse sermon on the consecration of a church remarked when he said that a church building signifies the whole congregation—the part of the congregation

Figure 2.11. The central pillar supporting the roof structure at Uvdal. The ceiling above it is an early modern modification which may contribute to better heat retention, but which prevents any sight of the branching of the rafters away from the "tree trunk." The early-modern artist who decorated the church may have been aware of the Yggdrasil tradition, for he painted an enveloping and luxuriant spread of leaves and vines on the ceiling and walls of the entire church. The central wooden stave or tree trunk structure used in Norway was paralleled by the central stone pillar design of the round churches on Bornholm in Denmark. Author's photograph.

which is in heaven and the part of it that is still on earth.[36] The vertical distance that suggests these two parts are separate but still connected may be the carved heads in the semidark distance atop the staves in Germanic, and in the horizontal it is the altar rail with its archway, the rood screen, or the chancel rail, as it is variously called, that suggests the separation and connection of those in heaven and those on earth.

As I walked into the vestibule of the Uvdal church, something there made my heart jump. It was a discarded screen, a portal carving just like the ones I had seen but completely different (Figure 2.12).

36. See Peter Anker and Paul Hamlyn, pp. 378–79.

Figure 2.12. Upper part of the openwork carved doorway between the nave and the sanctuary (the gate to the altar, chancel rail, or rood screen) found now in the vestibule of the Uvdal church. The leaves and vines are in peaceful swirls. A similar openwork sanctuary doorway, the top portion, can be seen still in position at Urnes. The small wooden block is a separator keeping the two protective plastic sheets apart. Author's photograph.

It had been carved all the way through, with open lattice work permitting light and sound to come through. It was protected by two sheets of very heavy plastic, and I could see why, as opposed to the portal carvings I had seen, this one was only about an inch and a half or so thick. It had been mistakenly used and abused by being placed outside as part of a new south entrance centuries ago and was now weather beaten, but still remarkably whole. When I looked I knew from the openwork carving, the complete absence of snakes and of any other animals, and a total absence of violence, just intertwined foliage and the slender lines of vines, that this had been the portal to the sanctuary.[37] Under this portal, which had been part of the chancel rail, the rood screen, had been the ritual, inner doorway between the heavenly and earthly sections of the stave church. And it depicted nothing but a pure vine. Since it was an open carving, the lights, the movements, glimpses of gold and white vestments and vessels, chalice and paten, could be seen. The chanting of the choir could be heard as well through the open sanctuary doorway and its surrounding open, latticework portal with the leaves and tendrils of the vine. This entrance way to "heaven" goes far beyond the portal of the entrance and leads the Norse Christian to the treasure place of peace and protection. It says, "I am the vine, you are the branches." Through this doorway comes Communion with the Vine and with the rune-staves of the Gospel, Christ himself speaking in the language of the storytellers of Yggdrasil.

What would Mass have been like in a stave church 800 years ago? There is a Swedish altar tapestry[38] that gives a hint. We can imagine a congregation that comes to the church on horseback, bringing cattle with them for a feast as Pope Gregory suggests, bells from the church sounding down the valley, perhaps with the bifrost glowing over the mountains reminding that there is a road to Asgard. Some

37. See also *Uvdal Stavkirke Forteller,* Nils Friis, ed. (Uvdal: Nore og Uvdal kommune, 1992), pp. 8, 13. The lead article by Håkon Christie, "Kirkebygnings historie" to which this refers, agrees with this assessment and also contains a fine schematic of the church's earliest appearance, with diagrams showing the massive central post rising through the apse and ceiling to support the bell tower structure.

38. This can be found in Aron Anderson and Paul Hamlyn, *The Art of Scadinavia,* vol. 2 (London and New York: Hamlyn, 1970), illus. pp. 334, 248–49; interp. 391.

may be rowing their way across an icy fjord. They are well bundled up, not just for the journey, for in the church they have to provide their own heat. They gather in the covered ambulatory before the door is opened, since to open and close it frequently during the service would be hard on those trying to be warm inside. In the grayish light and torches they can see flickering images of the deer and the fighting serpents on the doorway. Then they go inside together, perhaps some with distant and comfortable thoughts of Lif and Lifthrasir, and stand among the tall tree trunks, women on one side, men on the other. In the midst of the people stands an enormous pillar, a reinforcing tree trunk spreading up into the branching rafters and darkness.

The altar piece at Uvdal suggests that many a priest or minister must have used this situation to preach about Adam and Eve with the tree of Eden between them. All around the upper staves the x-forms with their leaf decorations suggest live branches in the candlelight. The dim faces of long ago and of other stories look down from the stave tops. The very high sills and thresholds, the tightly joined wall staves, tongue and groove, keep the warmth of people in, and snow, rain, and cold out. The splendid gold vestments, the chant, and the incense would assure everyone that they who had been baptized with water were in as magic a place as they had been before Christ came, when it was the Norns who splashed water and mud on the tree.

And then at length when the moment of the consecration of the bread and wine came, the priest visible in the light of many candles, through the sanctuary doorway and screen, chanting the words of Christ from beyond the rood screen, "Take this all of you and eat it, this is my body which will be given up for you," a small bell begins ringing in the sanctuary, pealing out through the spaces in the vine carvings to the congregation. Its sound is taken up by the men surrounding the tree trunk in the middle of the church as they begin pulling on the ropes to set the two small bells up in the bell turret on the roof clanging (Figure 2.13). This is then taken up by the huge bells outside the church in the bell tower whose notes resound in deep-toned harmony with those on the roof, and as the congregation prays, with differing tempos the sounds of all the bells reverberate through the church and its staves and echo up and down the valley.

The twelfth-century altar tapestry from the church at Skog is unique in that it shows all this, a stave church in x-ray form, and perhaps a little bit more. In the center of the tapestry is a stave church,

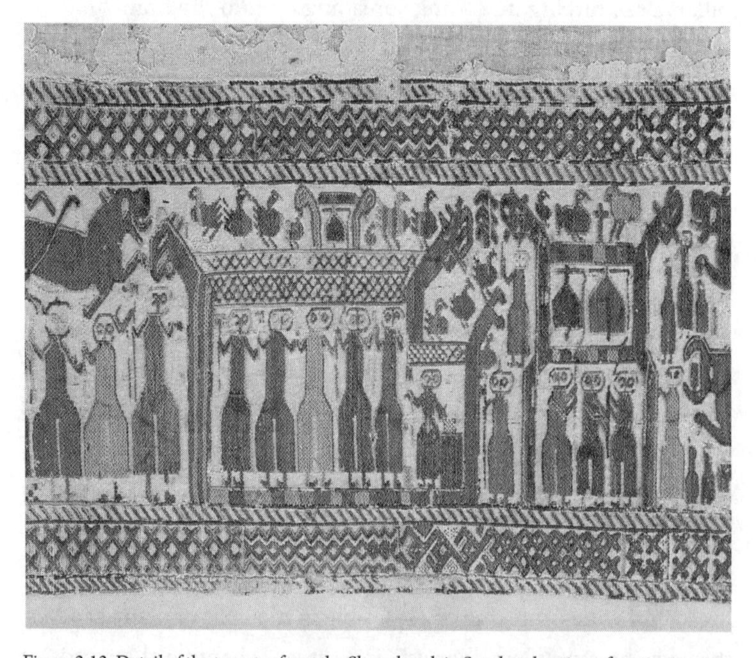

Figure 2.13. Detail of the tapestry from the Skog church in Sweden showing a functioning stave church. There are serpent heads at the eaves, the small bell tower above, a priest in the apse and the people in the nave with hands uplifted. The priest is pointing to the veiled chalice and ringing a sanctuary bell, as two members of the congregation pull on the roof bell tower rope. Outside to the right of the church, three more men are pulling the ropes to ring the much larger bells in the separate bell tower. From the Museum of National Antiquities, Stockholm. Werner Forman/Art Resource, New York.

depicted with the snake heads projecting left and right from the roof, the congregation inside in the nave. To the right, in the sanctuary part of the church barred off by the sanctuary rail, the priest is pointing to a partially covered chalice with one hand and is ringing a small sanctuary bell with the other. Inside the congregation, the second person from the right is pulling the rope to ring the small bell in the roof tower. Outside is the large bell tower, also equipped with the snake heads on the roof ends and with a cross on the roof, and inside are two very large bells, one of them so large that it takes two men to pull the bell rope.

The church is surrounded by crowds of people and animals coming to it. On the right end of the tapestry, men are arriving and dismounting from their horses. One has brought an ox. To the left of the church three more are about to enter the church, many animals are approaching, and some sort of three-headed monster with dogs barking at it is heading away. The artist uses feet significantly to indicate direction. The most fascinating part of the tapestry is the left end; nowadays it is often used for book illustrations on Norse topics. It depicts three very large figures, who have been identified variously as the three fates, as Woden, Thor, and Frey, and most recently as three king saints: St. Olaf, St. Erik, and St. Canute. The recent identification of the three as saints is again an attempt to avoid seeing Christian artists speaking in "pagan" language. Aron Anderson, mentioned above, does recognize some of the difficulties with seeing the three figures as saints, but throws up his hands at interpreting the scene. It is only necessary to recall Pope St. Gregory's letter on the use of pagan temples, as well as the spiritual manner of speaking of the stave churches, and I think we can say the three are not saints. The absence of halos is one thing, even more important is their feet. (See Figure 2.14.) They are all walking away from the church.

Figure 2.14. Detail of the Skog tapestry showing the gods leaving. From the Museum of National Antiquities, Stockholm. Werner Forman/Art Resource, New York.

As the three large figures walk away from the church on a special carpet or dais, their dogs trotting below express their attitudes—they are leaving with perfect composure. The figure on the left has only one eye, and is carrying a battle weapon, the figure in the middle is holding a hammer, and the figure on the right is holding what looks like a sheaf of wheat. Woden, Thor and Frey or Freya. (There does not seem to be a thread, or a well, present, and so I do not think they can be the Norns.) Then there is the curious matter of the shape of the crowns. In each case they look like twigs from a tree. Are Woden, Thor, and Frey spirits of the forest who are now returning to the woods whence they came? Next to Woden there is a tree, looking rather like an evergreen. Is it Yggdrasil, the Awesome One's Horse? The three gods are leaving peacefully, and quite contentedly, in this artist's representation, perhaps because they are leaving Yggdrasil's temple in the hands of Christians and Christ, for whom they prepared the way by embodying ancient stories of wisdom, strength, and happiness—and by helping all to remember the deep roots of Mimir's old and hopeful story that salvation would come in the form of a tree. It did. And then they left, graciously leaving their stave house to Christ.

Chapter 3

Bornholm's Round Churches and Baptismal Font

Bornholm is a medium-sized island in the Baltic Sea at about the latitude of Northumbria in northern England. It is approximately a parallelogram in shape, and is situated between the southern coast of Sweden and the northern coast of Germany and Poland. The island belongs to Denmark, as it did in the days when Christianity first came to it across the sea from Danish Scania, now southern Sweden, during the eleventh century. Bornholm is roughly 25 miles in length and about 19 miles across, with a comfortable, sun-filled climate in the summer at least, and a fairly constant sea breeze coming from the west. Like all islands, it has an isolation about it which lends to the persistence of many older things and usages in language and in architecture which may have long disappeared elsewhere. Among these older and fascinating things on Bornholm are four medieval round churches at Nyker, Olsker, Nylars, and Østerlars, as well as a heavy, stone baptismal font at Aakirkeby. All of these have, I believe, a special and remarkable kinship to the medieval stave churches of Norway.

Between the years 1150 and 1250, commencing therefore about one hundred years after the time of Bornholm's initial stages of conversion to Christianity, fifteen churches were built on the island,[1]

1. *The Old Churches of Bornholm*, ed. and text, Ann Vibeke Knudsen (Rønne, Bornholm: The Bornholm Museum, 1999), p. i.

Figure 3.1. The Nykirke on Bornholm seen from the east. The rounded apse is nearest the viewer, followed by the small choir ("song house" on Bornholm), and then the rounded drum and conical roof of the nave. The smaller vestibule to the left is a later addition. Author's photograph.

eleven in rectangular Romanesque[2] style, and four in a unique type of round shape (Figure 3.1). Their somewhat late date of origin shows that they may not be solely aimed at the conversion of "pagan" Germanic believers, but may just as well be the results of already converted Christians envisioning some harmony between their new faith and the old. The oldest Norwegian stave church, at Urnes, is dated to 1130–1150, and thus may be a bit older than those on Bornholm, but the other stave churches mentioned in the preceding chapter, including the one at Borgund, date from the period from 1150–1250—they are contemporaries of Bornholm's

2. *Romanesque* is used here as it is often in the literature on Bornholm's churches, with an emphasis on time period and tripartite construction: a long plain rectangular nave, joined to a smaller sanctuary at the east end, which consists of both a square or rounded choir and a semicircular apse for the altar; basilica style.

round churches. Both stave church and round church seem to have the contemplative aim of envisioning the new faith in concord with the poetic images of the old. In order to compare stave churches and round churches, however, it is necessary to take into account that a transfer of material from wood to stone was made—with a concomitant transfer of the image of Yggdrasil from the outside to the inside of the building.

Before considering the round churches themselves, however, I would like to begin this chapter, as might be considered ecclesiastically appropriate, with baptism, specifically with the renowned baptismal font at Aakirkeby (Figures 3.2a). The church at *Aa* (river, brook), the Aakirke, or "River Church," is so called from its position between two brooks, but its dedication provides the actual name of the church, which was given at the time of construction in the late eleventh century: the church of St. John the Baptist. The dedication of the main administrative church on Bornholm to John the Baptist may have persuaded the local church authorities to send to the island of Gotland to commission an extraordinary baptismal font in honor of the saint.[3] The master sculptor Sigraf must have been known at the time for his ability with baptismal fonts, based on the several which are still in use on Gotland. The images of two of these earlier fonts can be seen on the web; they seem to reflect an earlier and incomplete stage of the integrated masterwork that Sigraf sent to the Aakirke.[4]

When I walked into the church at Aakirkeby, a baptism was taking place. The minister wore the black gown and the large white ruff around the neck that gave an immediate feel of the sixteenth century,

3. Several other baptismal fonts on Bornholm were also brought from Gotland, but they are much plainer and cannot be compared to the one at Aakirkeby. In Norway, several of the medieval fonts in the stave churches are hollowed, vertical tree trunks.

4. Two that can be found on the Internet are the font at the Eke kyrke and the Lau kyrke.

but the baptism and the font spoke of much earlier times. When the ceremony was over, I was able to examine the font closely. The very first thing that an observer, or a candidate for baptism, sees, is the sculpted frieze of eleven arcaded pictures surrounding the upper bowl of the font. Eleven images are arranged in an arcade depicting the birth and death of Jesus Christ, and thus depicting for the baptismal candidate the life and death into which he or she is about to be immersed. As one circles the font counterclockwise, one can see each of the events sculpted in its own panel and identified by the sculptor in the dialect of Gotland in runic letters carved into the framework that marks off each scene.[5] There are eight scenes in bas-relief devoted to the story of the nativity, and only three to the Crucifixion. Moreover, fully five of the eight scenes of the nativity are devoted to the Magi. It is obvious that the coming and going of the three gentile kings is of major importance to the sculptor in his establishing an interpretive context for the convert's parallel approach to the font for baptism. In the three passion scenes, Sigraf's selection of the scourging of Christ at a wooden pillar, and Christ's being led to the nails and hammer for crucifixion, while the cross oversees the scene, sets the sculptor's own accent on the events, pointing to the importance of the tree in the passion of Christ.

Here are the runic captions on the font as given in English in the explanatory parish booklet.[6] My comments are in brackets:

1. "This is St. Gabriel, who said to Mary that she should bear a child."
2. "This is Elizabeth and Mary greeting each other."

5. The captions are done in the frame of each scene, much in the style used by Nicholas of Verdun on his Verdun altar at Klosterneuburg, except of course that Sigraf does not use Latin but the Germanic language and runic script of the baptismal candidate.
6. *AA Kirke (River Church) Bornholm*, Karsten Thorborg, H. C. Lorentzen, trans. (Rønne, Bornholm: Folkekirkens Menighedsråd, 2011).

3. "Here Mary is resting, having born the child, maker of heaven and earth, who redeemed us."
   [This panel is quite touching since it shows Mary exhausted, and Joseph as well, and he is holding her with both arms from the bottom of the bed. Above the two, the baby Jesus is in the crib, the ox and ass are above, an angel from heaven is censing on the left, and in parallel to him, the Magi's heavenly star is shining on the right.]
4. "These are the three Kings who first made offerings to Our Lord."
   [There is no panel for the shepherds in the fields at Christmas, though there are five images for the Magi. The poet is suggesting an identification of the catechumen, or of the person approaching the font for baptism, with the three kings, who found their way to Jesus despite being born in a land very far away. The Magi had no singing angels as did the shepherds, but significantly for the northern baptismal candidate, followed their own religious tradition, using astrology and the star risen in the east, to make the journey to Jesus Christ. Sigraf is here very close to the *Heliand*'s ecumenical and pagan-friendly presentation of the Magi as parallel to the situation of northern European Christians.][7]
5. "Here Our Lord received the offerings of the three Kings."
   [The offering of their gifts takes two panels. The kings approach humbly on foot, and the first king is already receiving a blessing from the child Jesus, who has two fingers extended in benediction.]

7. *The Heliand, The Saxon Gospel*, pp. 21–27.

Figure 3.2a. The baptismal font in the Aakirke on Bornholm. Above the three kings bring their gifts to the baby Jesus seated on his mother's lap. Below, the vines and intertangled life forms of Yggdrasil. The cloth left on the top left of the font is from a baptism that had just been done. Author's photograph.

6, 7, 8. "Here the three Kings rode away after having offered [their presents] to Our Lord."

[Each king gets a separate panel in the arcade. Their attitude expresses a certain happiness—done through the depiction of their horses, for the kings are now mounted and each horse is prancing with an upraised foreleg. Moreover, and this is the sculptor's important addition to the Gospel story as found in Matthew 2, the kings have received presents in return; they are carrying them in their hands. (We will return to this later, for I think this ties the whole composition together.)]

9. "The Jews took Our Lord and bound him to a tree and put him under surveillance."

[Sigraf has again made a significant change here; traditionally this scene in the passion is referred to as "the scourging at the pillar." The sculptor-poet has changed the stone pillar to a wooden pole, so that the whipping of Jesus occurred as a part of his being bound to the wood of a tree.]

10. "Then they took him and led him away."
    [I do not know the degree to which the *Heliand* might have had influence here, but in the panel it seems that he is being led in heavy rope or chain, which in the *Heliand* reflects the Saxon author's efforts to make the captivity of Jesus similar to the Saxons' own when the Christian Franks chained those who resisted baptism. Was there something similar done in the Baltic?]
11. "And here the Jews nailed Jesus to the cross. Look at this!"
    [In this panel Jesus is blessing the hammer and nails which are being shown to him, and in the background, directly under the central arch of the panel, stands the wooden tree, the cross. The cross itself is the central focus; Jesus is not shown on it but approaching it, so that the observer can be urged by the artist to pay attention to the importance of the central object in this scene. It is at this point, after urging the observer to look carefully, Sigraf signed his work by writing "Master Sigraf." The next scene, if one continues walking around the font, will be the Annunciation. And so one is returned from contemplating death to life beginning.]

Now the observer has to look at the base of the font. It is completely different, and the parish booklet mentioned above is not enthusiastic. "There is a certain discrepancy between the message of the Christian bowl and the heathen features of the foot, also in style." It then offers a moral interpretation, "Probably signifying that man by baptism overcomes the evil forces." Let us take a closer look at the foot or base of the font. I believe the base is quite closely and positively tied to the bowl. As a matter of fact, Sigraf has suggested as much by the woven rope that he has sculpted around the spot where the bowl and the base are joined. That woven cord between the two is as much a signal of intent and a signature as the "Sigraf" put in runes on the last column above.

While moving around the font or simply standing in front of it, it is impossible not to notice the four living creatures that project from the base. One may be tempted to assume that they are the traditional four animals of Matthew, Mark, Luke, and John, but they are not. There are two lions, a ram, and a human being. Both the lions and also the human being have a section of the body of a long snake in their mouth which they are biting. The ram is presumably more interested in eating the vegetation. The serpent turns out to be an entwinement of more than one serpent, and at their tails the snakes transform into vines, leaves, and flowers. This is the familiar type of depiction of the tree of life, Yggdrasil, which we saw in Norway. Modern depictions of Yggdrasil imagine its trunk and branches more in the Tree's cosmic role as the central support and scaffolding for the worlds. Medieval depictions are impressed with the Tree's living creatures devouring other living things, transforming life through eating and being eaten into still other creatures, as animals become plants and plants animals, and death reciprocates with life. In this form Yggdrasil can be found around the portals of the Norwegian stave church; and it is also in this life-based manner that Yggdrasil is described in the Edda.

The Tree is standing steady and suffering but teeming with the necessary violence of the cycle of life: deer gnawing at its side, the Nidhogg serpent biting at its roots, and innumerable snakes forever biting at its branches and striking at the deer that eat the branches.[8]

In this sense one can see why the artist put only scenes of birth and death from Christ's life around the bowl. The mystery of the Incarnation is that the Son of God came down from heaven to join in human beings' life and death, eating animals and vegetation, to be a part of existence in the universe, the cosmic tree. In other words, in the concepts of Germanic myth, Christ lived in the branches of Yggdrasil as we do, and died there, as Sigraf hinted with his creation of a wooden pole for the scourging, and in calling attention to the wooden cross by placing it by itself in the middle of his depiction of the Crucifixion. The wooden cross of Christ is situated above the leaves, flowers, and fruit of Yggdrasil, as if it constitutes a significant part of their fulfillment. And, as he hinted with the immediately subsequent depiction of the Annunciation, Christ will take up life again.

I got down onto the floor of the church because I wanted to see more clearly what was sculpted on the undersurface of the bowl. Underneath, on the bottom surface of the bowl, there is no sight of the violence of life, nor of human beings and lions and sheep and vinelike snakes, eating and being eaten; underneath the bowl, the tree of life surges up from the base to become a powerful and peaceful vine, unfolding itself in flower, acanthus leaves, and great seed pods. The peaceful side of the natural tree of life thus visibly supports the bowl and the water of the baptismal font in its task of giving the fulfillment of life—that is, a

8. See the *Elder Edda, Grimnismal,* pp. 33–35; in Carolyne Larrington's translation, *The Poetic Edda* (New York/Oxford: Oxford University Press, 1996), pp. 56–57.

Figure 3.2b. The passion and Crucifixion panels on the bowl of the font above, and below on the base of the font a lion is biting on a snake, whose tail is becoming a plant with a flower. Author's photograph.

life beyond, but connected to, the natural cycle of life symbolized by Yggdrasil (Figure 3.2b). I remembered how the violence of the portals on the stave churches became a peaceful, sound- and light-transmitting vine at the chancel gate to the sanctuary in the church in Uvdal. And a similar chancel gateway at Urnes is still in place leading to the altar. The living vine of the tree of life, the "awesome horse"[9] that supports life in the nine worlds, also supports the waters of baptism.

Appropriately for a baptismal font, Yggdrasil is also connected to water. It is not only the holy place where the gods gather in

9. The absence of a possessive "s" at the end of "Ygg-" in the name Yggdrasil has occasioned some scholars to question the common understanding of Ygg-drasil as "the Awesome One's Horse," [i.e.,"Woden's Horse"]. Since the word "Ygg" might also be construed as referring to "drasil," the tree itself, perhaps the name was also understood as "The Awesome Horse."

counsel under its branches, but it is near the water of Urd,[10] the well of time past, from which the Norns[11] gather loam and water to splash on the great evergreen tree's trunk and thereby give it continuing life. The sculptor has realized that the waters of the Christian font poured, not by the Norns but by the priest of the White Christ,[12] also grant continuation in life to every person living in it who, like the Magi, approaches to be splashed with its water for continuance of life after death. The story of Yggdrasil, the water of time, and the dew from the branches, sustaining and protecting Life[13] and Lifthrasir, are treated as truly prophetic and are shown to have been fulfilled.

And with that we are back to the question that I left unanswered several pages back. Why is so much attention given to the Magi who follow their religion's starlore to find their way to Christ? The Germanic people of the North are also gentiles; they are also without Torah or prophets to guide them, except that instead of following a storied star to find Jesus on his mother's lap, they follow their religion's lore of the sacred tree which locates the place from which the water of life and fate flows as being at the base of Yggdrasil. And that is why it is appropriate that Yggdrasil be depicted on the base of the Aakirke's baptismal font.

10. Also *Wurd*, and *Wyrd*, and the origin of the modern English "weird."

11. The three Norns are Urd, Verdandi, and Skuld, or "what came to pass," "what is coming to pass," and "what shall come to pass." They personify fate and time which determine the lives and course of events of men. They have knowledge of the past, the present, and the future. It is they who write the runes on tree staves for fortune telling. Cf. H.R. Ellis Davidson, *Gods and Myths of Northern Europe* (New York: Penguin, 1964), pp. 26, 195. I translate their names, however, based more on the verb *werden*, "to become" and skuld on the future auxiliary "shall."

12. Possibly so called from the white garment worn by Christ, also worn liturgically by an officiating priest (the alb) and ritually given to the catechumen during baptism.

13. "Lif" and in some translators' versions "Life," which is the meaning of *Líf*. "Lifthrasir" is unclear, but may mean something like "Life-propagator," or as Andy Orchard's new translation has it: "Life-eager." Cf. his *The Elder Edda, A Book of Viking Lore* (London/New York: Penguin, 2011) p. 47.

As a part of the ritual of baptism, the candidate must first renounce Satan and all his works and declare himself a believer in the Father, the Son, and the Holy Spirit. We know from the Saxon baptismal oath of the ninth century that Germanic pagans were required to abjure not just Satan, but also specifically to renounce Thor, Woden, and in this case their own Saxnot.[14] Significantly, church authorities did not see fit in Saxony (or Scandinavia) to add Yggdrasil to that list. If they had, Yggdrasil most certainly would not have found its way to the base of a baptismal font in a near-cathedral church. Yggdrasil must have been regarded in a more neutral light, as a commonly accepted, more scientific and story-telling description of the universe, with its fate, its growth, its passage of time—sovereign entities in their way—but nothing satanic, or religiously threatening, no personal deity standing in opposition to the ultimate sovereignty of the Trinity.

But what of the Magi as archetypes? Sigraf has them all prancing away, high on their horses, each one given his own frame in the composition, and quite content (Figure 3.3). Look carefully at their hands. When they arrived they had their gold, frankincense, and myrrh in their hands. In Matthew's Gospel story nothing is mentioned about them receiving any presents in return. Sigraf has imagined a reciprocation on the part of Christ. Each one of the three kings is holding a long branch upright in his hand as he trots along. They have each been given, in return for their coming to the newborn Christ, a branch of the undying tree of life for themselves, perhaps to take back home and plant. What a beautiful way

14. "*End ec forsacho allum dioboles uuercum and uuordum, Thunaer ende Uuoden ende Saxnote ende allum them unholdum the hira genotas sint.*" [And I renounce all the devil's works and words, Thor, Woden and Saxnot, and all those fiends that are their companions]. The Tree of Life must not be among that number. Cf. "The Old Saxon Baptismal Vow" on the web under that title, and Rudolf Simek, *Dictionary of Northern Mythology* (Cambridge: D. S. Brewer, 1996), p. 276.

Figure 3.3. Detail of the basin of the font, the Magi leaving to return to their own country. In a nonbiblical addition, but in conformacy with Yggdrasil as tree of life at the base of the baptismal font, each one of the three kings is returning with a branch in his hand. Author's photograph.

to say how the Magi were enriched by their visit to their generous gift-giving Lord, and to say it in the language of Germanic mythology! What a beautiful way to speak to the catechumen or candidate for baptism who is coming to the baptismal water from the religious context of Nordic mythology, and to describe to him or her what is happening at the font in a mixture of Christian and Germanic story so that he can realize where he is and what he is receiving.

It is not surprising then that in the round churches on Bornholm the place of the baptismal fonts was on a line between the north (women's) and the south (men's) entrances, at the very foot of the large central column that supported the church.[15] And this brings us to the round churches.

15. See Elaine Treharne's "Rebirth in the *Dream of the Rood*" in *The Place of the Cross in Anglo-Saxon England*, eds. Catherine Karkov, Sarah Larratt Keefer, and Karen LouiseJolly (Rochester, NY: The Boydell Press, 2006), pp. 145–57.

The **round churches** are one of the chief sites on the island that visitors and tourists want to see. It is often said that these four churches are unique because of their round shape, but this is not really the case. Round, or more usually, octagonal churches, could be found easily then and now in Denmark and Sweden, as well as the Temple Church in London, Charlemagne's palatine chapel in Aachen, St. Michael in Fulda, Santo Stefano Rotondo in Rome, Justinian's San Vitale in Ravenna, as well as the mother church of all churches of this design, Constantine's Church of the Holy Sepulcher in Jerusalem. To enter such a church is to enter analogously into the tomb of Christ, the place of the Resurrection.[16] Bornholm's round churches really are unique, however, but primarily for another and more important reason: they have a single, very imposing, central pillar rising like a huge and spreading tree trunk in the middle of the circular nave. This is unique.[17] No other round or octagonal church in Europe or Palestine, to my knowledge, has such a structure. Bornholm's round churches really should be called *central pillar round churches.* It is to the interpretation of these central pillars and to their encircling frescoes and umbrella-like ceilings that I would like to turn my attention.

A great deal of local scholarship seems to have been devoted to the study of the possible military and storage function of the second and third floors (the Nykirke has only two stories) of the circular nave. My purpose will be to explore the meaning of the first floor, the worship space of the church, considering them in analogy to the stave churches, and by interpreting the meaning of the central pillar.

16. For this reason it was also the shape often chosen for baptisteries.

17. They are thus no argument for the presence of the Templar-style churches on the island as proposed by Erling Haagensen and Henry Lincoln.

When one approaches a round church like the **Nykirke** [New Church],[18] officially known as All Saints Church, it is quite different than the first sight of a Norwegian stave church. Whereas the stave church makes an immediate and complex impression with its rising tiers of roofs, serpent heads on the upper gables, crosses on the lower ones, the round church by contrast is the image of simplicity. From afar one sees both the high, black, conical roof and the plain, low, round silo-like building beneath it. A black cone on a white drum—and of roughly equal height—it is almost modern art. The whitewash on the outside is a modern innovation, however. In the Middle Ages the exterior wall of the circular nave would have been the natural gray-brown color of its construction from fieldstone. With the stone's natural color, there might have been some resemblance to an evergreen tree with a very wide brown trunk, and the projecting kingpin at the top of the long conical roof might have also suggested general shape and especially the top of a spruce as with the stave churches' roofs and kingpin, but I think the analogy might have been a bit obscure. The black of the roof, however, would have been there if the oak shingles on the roof were tarred as they were and are in Norway. In any case, the simplicity of the form of the exterior[19] does not give as clear and unambiguous a suggestion of an evergreen tree.

Approaching the portal, one is once again confronted with a simplicity that contrasts with the tangle of snakes and vines and deer and bears that can be found on the Norwegian stave church's portal. There is a weapons room, or *vapenhus,* a vestibule adjoining the

18. The New Church could be so named because it was the latest built of the four round churches. Possibly, however, it could be "new" in contrast to the older, rectangular Knutskirke, [St. Canute's Church] built sometime after 1104 and likely the first stone church on the island. The Nykirke would then be "new church" by reason of chronology and the new, round style.
19. This simplicity is best seen in the Nykirke. The other churches are higher and often required the addition of large external buttresses to keep the top of the walls from sagging outward.

south portal where the men deposit their weaponry before entering the church, as with the ambulatory space in Norway. The doorway itself, however, is quite plain.

Entering the church is a shock, or at least it was for me. As you open the door you are immediately confronted with an enormous pillar in the center of the room (Figure 3.4). I had expected one, of course, but its sheer girth was overawing and the sheer amount of space it took up in the room proclaimed loudly that it was the central feature of the church. Coming in and standing next to it, you feel dwarfed; then looking up, you can see that it is not a classical pillar with fine and narrow proportions with a well-defined and separate capital and base. The massive pillar simply continues up and, after a small lip, begins to fan out on all sides. It does not

Figure 3.4. Nykirke, interior. The massive central pillar in the nave that greets the visitor on entrance into the church. The frieze around the top of the pillar depicts the passion, death, and resurrection of Christ. Author's photograph.

rise up in a narrowing column to terminate a capital, which then acts to supports the ceiling; instead it curves up and out and becomes the overarching ceiling, gradually descending at the end of its arc to meet the circular outside wall at all points. The column branches out in all directions to become an arched umbrella-like ceiling for the congregation which stands around and beneath it. The pillar and its overhead create a safe, centered, overshadowed space, endowed with a feeling of security and protection. This is the effect of having a ring-shaped barrel vault which rests its inside edge on the powerful central pillar and its outside edge on the building's outer wall—the function of Yggdrasil's powerful trunk and branches architecturally expressed. In addition, one of the oldest drawings of the church, made in 1756, shows the baptismal font still at the foot of the pillar on the western side: the well of water in front of the tree. Thus in the language of Germanic myth, one is invited to realize that one has entered holy space, and is standing where gods gathered and the Norns sprinkle, the place which will offer rescue and protection. The wood of the tree will shield the last living man and woman against the final fire [Surt] and all forces that will bring about Ragnarok in the attempt to destroy all life and all the worlds. Snorri makes this important point in his prose Edda, and to back it he cites the ancient wisdom of the Vafthrudnismal in the Elder Edda:

> And in a place called Hoddmimir's holt [Yggdrasil] two people will lie hid during Surt's fire, called Life and Lifthrasir, and their food will be the dews of the morning. And from these people there will be descended such a great progeny that all the world will be inhabited. As it says here:
> Life and Lifthrasir, and they shall lie hid
> in Hoddmimir's wood,

they will have the morning dew for food;
from them the generations will spring.[20]

Then as one looks up at the fresco, one sees the pillar giving the identity of the place in the language of Christ's saga. The fresco is on the pillar itself, not on the walls, thus associating the column with what is depicted. The fresco of thirteen scenes winds its way around the top of the pillar telling the story of the crucifixion of Christ on the tree through to the Ascension. It begins with the scene of Judas kissing Christ in betrayal, a warning against infidelity, the first thing that a member of the congregations sees on entering through the men's (south) door. The frieze goes on beautifully to depict Jesus carrying the wood of the cross and his crucifixion on it, by simply doing the cross in spare outline (Figure 3.5). This lets the observer see the pillar through the cross, and so with the sparest of means the artist lets the observer associate the wood of Yggdrasil with the wood of the cross.

On the eastern side of the nave beginning with the chancel archway is the opening of the church to the east: the square choir and semicircular apse of the sanctuary. A later artist, perhaps of the sixteenth century, painted entwined vines with leaves, flowers, and stars on the underside of this arch, thus showing an awareness that the altar area is associated with the tree Yggdrasil. "I am the vine, you are the branches." This makes one go back and study the fresco around the pillar once more. The top and bottom border are a flourishing vine above and stylized ivy below, marking the passion as having occurred in the realm of Yggdrasil. Even more to the point, looking at each of the thirteen frames showing the passion of

20. Snorri Sturluson, *Edda*, Anthony Faulkes, trans. (London: Orion House, 1987 [Everyman, 1987]), p. 57. *The Poetic Edda*, Carolyne Larrington, trans. (New York/Oxford: Oxford University Press, 1996), p. 47.

Figure 3.5. Nykirke, detail of column. The panel depicts the events of the Crucifixion (the burial and Resurrection are to the right in the next panel) all as happening among the stars and between the vines of the Tree. The cross is only sketchily outlined, perhaps in order not to make it a thing different from the pillar itself. Author's photograph.

Christ, there are stars randomly shining in each scene, even around Pontius Pilate, and above each scene, the sun itself is shining down brightly and the quarter moon is marking off the passage of time. The presence of the stars and the twisting vegetation in the scenes of the passion are truly affecting. Jesus Christ died and rose within the nine worlds; walked on Midgard; and lived, suffered, and died in the branches of Yggdrasil as do plants, animals, and men. As the tree of the world turned, carrying the sun, moon, and stars of the world, they counted away the allotted days of Jesus's life. The Word became a human being and "pitched his tent among us"[21] it says most touchingly in northern cosmological poetry.

I can imagine a Christmas liturgy in this church, perhaps a midnight Mass in which amid the long enduring darkness of a northern winter, the warm candle lights, the golden chalice, and the smell of incense suggest the presence of the Magi not too far off. When the time for the chanting of the Christmas gospel arrives, the priest and his deacon come forth from the apse through the choir, as from heaven to earth, holding the shining gospel book aloft, processing under the archway from the sanctuary, to stand next to the great "tree trunk" in the middle of the church, and there opening the book they sing the nativity story of the coming of Christ from St. Luke. Christ has come from the heavenly sanctuary to the cosmic world of the tree of life, wrapped in swaddling and laid in a manger. . . . Then, circling the tree, amid moving candles and incense, the priest and deacon bring the golden gospel book back to the altar in the sanctuary from whence it had come.

Leaving the first floor for a moment, a stairway in the wall will take you to the second floor of the Nykirke. On the second floor, as in all the round churches, the central pillar continues up from below, through the floor to the ceiling, where it stops; and from its round top, rafter after rafter radiates out in a circle from to the outer wall, forming a base from which the struts and braces hold up the conical roof (Figure 3.6). The pillar is in the middle of the room, and the rafters radiating from it look distinctly like branches.[22] This

21. Jn. 1:14, "eskēnosen en hēmin."

22. Currently there is no access to the second floor; however, the Olskirke below can serve as a parallel for visualization.

might have been comforting for anyone who was using the second floor as a refuge, and remembering Yggdrasil's promise of protection. Nykirke does not have a third floor, and its second floor, if used as a refuge in time of pirate raids, would have been dependent on secure doors and its high small windows to prevent entrance. If someone did break down the door, the only way upstairs is by a single, narrow, very easily defended stairway inside the wall.

The **Olskirke** (St. Olaf's Church) has a third floor and looks perhaps as though it could serve as a refuge in an emergency, and could possibly mount a more active defense. It also has openings for very large timbers to bar the doors. However my main interest is the first floor, the church itself. Once again one must ask the question, how could a circular shape with a large central pillar serve the purposes of divine service, the Mass and baptism in particular? If

Figure 3.6. Olskirke, upper story. The radially placed rafters suggest a tree-like building on the inside, as does the cone-shaped roof they support when viewed from the outside. Author's photograph.

defense were the main consideration, one could also build a fortified rectangular basilical church, such as was certainly done in the majority of cases—the Knutskirke and the Rutskirke are examples. Both of these are very strongly built, with highly defensible, thick walls, small windows, and a front tower that is practically a keep. In the case of the rectangular Rutskirke, the remains of an outer wall and a defensible bell tower show that at least in the early days, it was quite possible to erect a rectangular church as a fully fortified refuge and fortress. Why then create a new circular style church? Once again I think we can go to the concept of speaking in the native language for at least part of an answer. The circular design may be an attempt to express the gospel in familiar northern terms,[23] an attempt to alter one's feelings of hostility, or that of one's neighbors, to the foreignness of the new religion into a more benevolent perception of its being familiar, even a fulfillment of the cosmology of the old Germanic religion. (And, of course, it doesn't hurt if the walls are thick!)

In the case of St. Olaf's Church, it is clear from the moment you walk in that the artist who did the ceiling of the nave realized what the church, and above all the central pillar, stood for, and he expressed it all over the ceiling—the tree of life, Yggdrasil (Figure 3.7). He may have worked quite some time after the church was finished, showing that the mythic meaning of the unusual structure carried down through generations. As you walk in and are confronted with a dusky central pillar, you can see immediately that it is the broad, central radiant point supporting the circular vault, whose curved ceiling overarches the church. What you see next is astonishing—all over the ceiling extending out from the top of the pillar in every direction are the familiar vines and tendrils of

23. Since the Second Vatican Council, the term used in theological circles for the effort at cultural accommodation of the gospel is "inculturation."

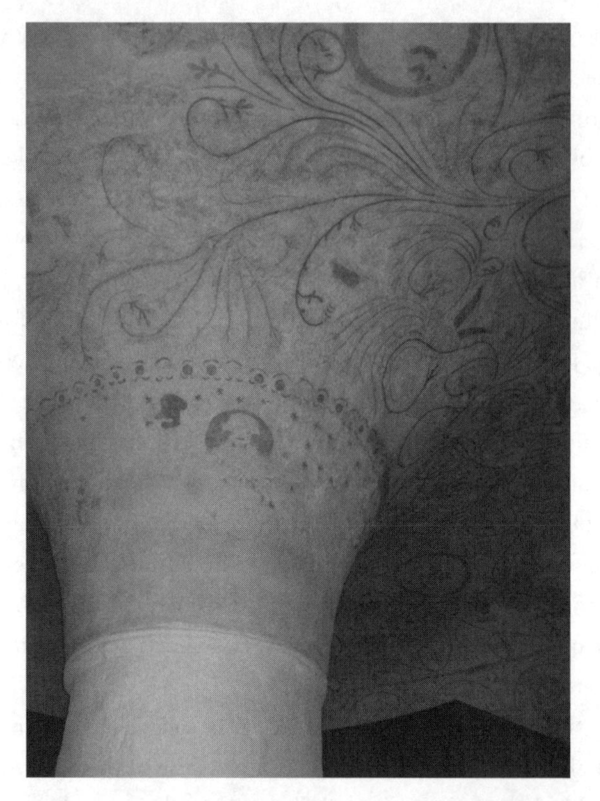

Figure 3.7. More than any other, this church's central pillar with its overhanging circular vaulting, all painted in vines, stars, constellations, even with evergreen pine (spruce) cones, gives the observer the feeling of standing under the protection of the Yggdrasil as the world tree. Author's photograph.

the tree of life, almost immediately bringing to mind Snorri's description of the upper part of Yggdrasil: "Of all trees [it is] the biggest and best. Its branches spread out over all the world and extend across the sky."[24] It is just what the congregation entering the church looks up and sees! The restorers have uncovered a wealth of detail, not all of which is clearly resolvable, but the overall effect

24. Sturluson, Snorri, *Edda*, Anthony Faulkes, trans. (London/Rutland, VT.: Dent, Everyman/Orion, 1987), p. 17.

Figure 3.8. Detail of the sweep of the vines and the top of the pillar as it arches over to the encircling side wall. The small brig hanging from the ceiling is a votive, a reminder to pray for those in peril on the sea, especially for those sailing from Bornholm. Author's photograph.

is sure. The congregation is sitting under the vines and branches of the evergreen world tree.[25]

Beginning at the lip at the top of the column, there are several images which are no longer clear, but are all interspersed with the stars of the sky. Above them a thin band shows a series of disks so arranged in two's that they circle the whole tree, possibly standing for the moon or sun. Above the band a riot of vinelike vegetation goes across the whole "sky" from the pillar to the outer wall, overshadowing the congregation (Figure 3.8). These vinelike branches contain circular open spaces for images which only in a few places

25. The theme of the cross as the tree of life from paradise can also be found on the great apsidal mosaic of the church of San Clemente in Rome, mentioned in the Introduction. It is also from the twelfth century. See Michael G. Sundell, *Mosaics in the Eternal City* (Tempe, AZ: Arizona Center for Medieval Studies, 2007), pp. 89–94.

have remained in good enough condition to be restored. One of them is a sort of dog-faced figure (below the circular disc belt), another (above) is a standing figure in a star filled circle holding a snake in his hand. My guess is that these are constellations, Canis Major possibly being the first, and Ophiuchus, the snake handler, the other. If so, it is good to see that the stars of heaven are seen as a part of the spreading branches of the world tree. They too are connected to the central tree trunk of the world and look down on the people in the church. At the bottom of the arched ceiling where it joins the wall are a series of small roundels encircling the church, whose scenes would be very interesting and rewarding to make out but unfortunately they have not been well preserved and may not be restorable. My guess is that rather than Old Testament scenes as has been suggested, they might represent objects or things from nature, constellations, and perhaps be connected to stories of Yggdrasil.[26]

When I saw this ceiling, I felt truly confirmed that the central pillar of the church was recognized, even generations after the construction of the building, as the trunk of the cosmic world tree. The ceiling painter provided mysterious colored pairs of carrotlike items among the vines. It took a while, and a moment of staring up at a tall spruce much later, to recognize what they must be: pine cones! The mysterious nature of the ceiling vines and the central trunk is given clearer identity through them—this is the evergreen world tree. If one goes up to the second story, one can see that it continues upward, providing another story for Yggdrasil-like protection for the women and children and church goods in time of a hostile raid, and on the third story not only are there apertures in the wall for possible fighting positions, but also the central "tree trunk" again comes

26. There is a sailing vessel, a brig, hanging from the ceiling, something seen in churches all over the world among sailing communities, a prayer for safety.

Figure 3.9. The central pillar shows its relationship to the biblical trees in the Garden of Eden. Branches are above and below Adam and Eve on the frieze as they are asked by God to leave. They are walking but clutching their fig leaves. The mixed red and white apples are on the tree of the knowledge of good and evil. The author is standing below them. The panel directly above me had deteriorated too much to be restored. Author's photograph.

to an end with radiating beams, "branches" providing a foundation for the roof above[27] as well as protection for the people below.

27. The current conical roof of the churches is thought to date from the late Middle Ages. They may have been designed to suggest the notion of the church as the evergreen Yggdrasil, but the earliest roof here may have been flat for military purposes, with wall holes for the

The **Nylarskirke** (St. Nicholas' Church) has a central pillar with the common architectural characteristic of the others, the circling barrel vault, and the fresco around the pillar shows that the artist realized indeed that it is a tree trunk, and possibly Yggdrasil, but he associates it with the biblical tree of life (and the tree of the knowledge of good and evil) in the Garden of Eden. The fresco around the "capital" of the pillar tells the story of Adam and Eve, featuring the two trees (Figure 3.9). This gives an identity and a location to the congregation standing about the pillar, they are in the primal human position of Adam and Eve in the Garden of Paradise when they are in the church, and thus encouraged to remember the primal sin of man—wanting to be like God, eating from the forbidden tree. They are also reminded of the other tree in the Garden of Eden: the tree of life. The cross and altar in the apse, reminds them by parallel that through Christ they have been given the once forbidden fruit of the tree of life, the bread and wine of his life from the tree of the cross. In the Nylarskirke this parallel has been nicely recreated in modern times by the erection of a large cross which can be seen from the congregation by looking past Adam and Eve's tree of life in its midst, to the sanctuary area where the altar stands on which the cross rests.

The artist has taken advantage of his poetic realization that the central pillar is a tree from Eden by two small and insightful additions. Each one of the apples hanging on the tree of the knowledge of good and evil is half red and half white,[28] as is also the serpent coiled around the tree, who is white but with a long red stripe running the length of his body. The serpent does not have the head of a

construction of hoardings on the outside of the wall. These holes, however, as those at the top of the Norwegian stave churches, also provided then and now for a necessary strong updraft of air to keep excess moisture from settling on the wooden beams and causing rot.

28. This is also the case in the Grimms' *Snow White*. The witch makes the apple in two halves of which only the red portion is poisoned. I do not know if the Grimms were aware of this fresco.

snake, but a human head and face. The second insight involves the famous fig leaves with which Adam and Eve cover their genitalia after having sinned. They are identical to the leaves the artist has drawn on the tree of life, suggesting sex and reproduction are not in liaison with the tree of sin but are related to the tree of life. The tree-pillar in the center of the church may have come from the North and be called Yggdrasil but the artist suggests it can also be found in the stories of Scripture. In the Bible it takes the form of the two trees of Genesis—but it is primarily—through the cross, and the church building it supports, and the congregation it protects—to be found in the tree of life, which is also significantly in the *middle* of the Garden of Eden.[29]

The **Østerlarskirke** (St. Lawrence Church) is the largest of the round churches and seems to have had an active defensive capability on its third story, perhaps more than the others whose upper stories seem more like secure places of refuge or storage—though there is no record of any battle activity at the church.[30] The liturgical area, the first floor, of the church, is unique among the four round churches in that its central pillar can actually be entered (see Figure 3.10).[31] This ability to be entered is, I believe, the defining characteristic of Østerlars church, associating it with Yggdrasil, the tree of rescue, on the day of Ragnarok. It surely occupies an enormous proportion of the nave: it is eighteen feet in diameter out of an internal church diameter of forty feet, therefore almost 50% of the diameter, leaving

29. For the history of the tradition of seeing the two trees of Eden as one, see Ann W. Astell, *Eating Beauty*, pp. 27–40.

30. Carl Nepper-Christensen, *The Church of St. Lawrence, A Brief Description of the Round Church of Østerlars*, Stuart Goodale, trans. (Allinge, Bornholm: Gornitzkas Bogtrykkeri, 1989), pp. 20–21.

31. It cannot, however, be ascended. There is no internal stairwell. It is not designed as a fighting space in case of break-in; the multiple doorways would make it militarily dangerous and indefensible. If the space were for defensive purposes it would have had fewer and smaller openings, and would have more solidly supported the sections of the tower above it.

a relatively narrow band around it, only about eleven feet wide, less than its own diameter, to accommodate the congregation. This pillar is hollow, pierced by all of six arched doorways, and both its size and its doorways must have been used for some ancillary but meaningful function during the Eucharist; certainly the presence and size of such a feature in the middle of the room make it something the priest could not ignore nor want to circumvent.

The central tree trunk has its own vaulted ceiling within and fans out at the top to create a narrow circular barrel vault for the nave as with the other three churches. It is encircled on the outside by a frieze from about 1350 that associates the pillar with the life of Christ and especially with the last judgment. The artist certainly seems to have caught the allusion to Yggdrasil at Ragnarok created by the unique characteristics of the hollow pillar. Unlike the solid central pillars of the other three churches, it occupies an enormous portion of the round nave; and unlike the other central "tree trunks," it cannot easily be bypassed in moving about the nave. As a matter of fact, both the hollowness of the enormous "tree trunk" and the six arched doorways cut into it tell anyone present that it is designed to be entered. There is no Old Testament analogue for such a tree in Genesis.[32] Unlike the use of the Garden of Eden's trees on the frieze that we saw at Nylarskirke, the presence of six arched entries giving access into the interior of the spreading "tree trunk" says forcefully that rather than keeping people out, it was designed for multiple entry: Lif and Lifthrasir and all their human family. Thus the round church carries the same northern version of the message—Christ's offer of rescue-in-the-tree—as does the Norwegian stave church, but rather than being expressed in the carvings around the portal and in the overall external shape of the church with its rising gables

32. Perhaps Noah's ark might have been a distant possibility, but as an image it is too far from the tree, and I should imagine, rather difficult to erect as a church.

and snakes' heads, the saving evergreen tree at Østerlars is found within the stone church building. The central "tree trunk" carries the same invitation to enter the church and be saved from doomsday as do the portals at Urnes and Borgund, but extends the invitation in Yggdrasil-myth language within the church, through its six open portals inviting the candidate or believer to enter the rescuing central tree trunk.

What would the experience of Mass have been like at the Østerlarskirke with such a large hollow pillar in the middle of the church? I think the Mass would have begun with a procession from the western end of the church to the baptismal font, which would have been on the outside of the pillar on the western side. And then

Figure 3.10. Thanks to six large archways, the enormous central pillar at Østerlars is hollow and its interior is accessible at the base. This pillar thus allows communicants who are standing or are seated in the narrow circular nave, to make their approach to the altar for Communion in best northern style: by going into this central tree to find Christ and rescue in the sacrament within. Author's photograph.

preceded by cross and candles with incense, the priest and deacon would have gone through one of the portals of the "tree trunk" and would have emerged from one on the eastern, sanctuary, side and then gone under the chancel arch to the altar in the apse, thus demonstrating ritually what the function of the middle section is. The Gospel reading of the day would have been chanted under the chancel arch, and the sermon given from the same spot, with some movement from side to side so as to be seen and heard. A ready sermon would be right there in the frieze on the pillar: "Christ versus the Nidhogg serpent." Christ in the center of the frieze between the sun and the moon and seated on the rainbow bridge is blocking any of the good souls from being dragged into hel.[33] Hel here is depicted as the giant jaws of a snake, no doubt suggesting the association of going to hel with the Nidhogg serpent, devourer of corpses, eater of the roots of Yggdrasil. While two devils have wrapped a chain around a crowd of the damned, another is smiling at the congregation while exposing his derriere to it. On the other side of Christ, the just are emerging from their graves to walk toward him in perfect safety. The two swords that emerge from his mouth[34] are there to protect them, as the saints smile above both groups.

At Communion time, the congregation imitates the action of the just in the picture and walk in safety toward Christ. The protective "tree trunk" of Yggdrasil that kept Lif and Lifthrasir safe is between them and the body and blood of Christ, but it is not an obstacle—its archways are openings that facilitate passage. The hope of ultimate rescue and salvation is one the whole world and especially Christianity understand. The priest and the deacon walk from the altar area in the apse through the choir to stand in position

33. Hel or hell; I have used the Germanic "hel" to suggest the damp world of the Nidhogg serpent under the roots of the tree.

34. Rev. 1:16.

at a communion station just inside the central pillar. The men and women of the congregation walk through the portals of the tree and come to Him to receive the heavenly "dew of the morning." Turning and looking up at the fresco while waiting their turn, they might see Christ also emerging from his sepulcher in the panel next to his death on the tree. Then each one steps forward and approaches to receive Holy Communion with him into whose life and death they were once baptized at the font.

The base of that font at Aakirke was the world tree Yggdrasil with animals eating animal life and vines transforming themselves into flowers and fruit. On the upper basin of the font, the Magi walked toward the Mother and Child to offer their gifts, while the tree and the cross supported their coming and their going. Now as the communicant walks forward through the great tree of life to honor the Lord, each one receives in return their gift that can only be described as their branch of the tree of the life and death of Christ, to eat, to drink, and to return home—like Yggdrasil's vine, transformed.

The prophesy made long ago by the giant Vafthrudnis in the Poetic Edda has been fulfilled: protected and hidden in Hoddmimir's wood, the tree at the well, they will be fed with the morning dew.

Chapter 4

Entering Yggdrasil: The Viking Crosses at Middleton in Yorkshire

Looking at the two figured crosses from Viking-age Middleton (c. 930), it is helpful once again to remember the ninth-century *Heliand* (c. 830) and its remarkable poetic achievement of reexpressing the story of Christ in northern-European form a hundred years earlier. We cannot be sure of its direct influence on stave churches and on graveyard crosses, but the *Heliand* indirectly suggests a very useful and nearly contemporary way of approaching their unique iconographic style. The poem presents a religious style of representation that can move the observer away from trying to look at the Viking crosses with Mediterranean eyes, looking for standard biblical images, fairly literally reproduced. Christ as "Lord" is translated in the *Heliand* as *drohtin,* a chieftain, not a *dominus,* the influential head of a great Roman household. As "chieftain of mankind," his main duty becomes that of a Germanic chieftain to be a *mundboro,* to provide protection, *mund,* against enemies, and frequently in the poem Christ is referred to as *mahtic mundboro,* "powerful protector."

The *Heliand* exists today in two copies, one of which comes from ninth century Fulda, in Hessia, and the other, from mid-tenth century East Anglia, within the Danelaw, and thus its style of northern cultural accommodation of the gospel story may well bear on that expressed in the contemporary Middleton crosses. When I examined the East Anglian *Heliand* at the British Library, as mentioned, I was happy to find a Latin inscription[1] inside on the flyleaf identifying the copy as once having belonged to King Canute (Knut, Cnut; 995?—1035), whose Anglo-Scandinavian empire stretched from Norway, Sweden, and Denmark to England and the Isles, including of course the very area in the Danelaw where the crosses were found, Middleton in North Yorkshire. One wonders if Canute's copy of the *Heliand* could possibly have been a gift from his redoubtable and feisty mentor, Archbishop Wulfstan of York. Richard Fletcher gives something of the spirit of the times when he writes of Wulfstan's *Northumbrian Priests' Law:*

> Wulfstan was a realist who did not ask the impossible of his clergy. They must shave regularly, must not bring their weapons to church, must try to keep out of fights and must not perform in ale houses as 'ale minstrels.' It was expected that they would be married, but separations and second unions were forbidden. . . . They were to be on the lookout for heathen practices: divination, sacrifices, witchcraft, idol-worship, the veneration of holy trees or stones or wells, 'or any such nonsense,' as the archbishop robustly put it.[2]

1. "Quattuor Evangelia in lingua danica cum picturis deauratis: Liber quondã Canuti Regis." (Cot. Calig. A. vii). The description of the Saxon language of the *Heliand* as Danish may be further confirmation of the belief of contemporaries that the various Germanic speakers of England could comprehend each other and their continental cousins until Norman French arrived. The manuscript is in excellent condition, though the handwriting of the last part of it has the appearance of having been rushed, including initials drawn but, despite the "deauratis," above, not colored in.
2. *The Barbarian Conversion, From Paganism to Christianity* (Berkeley: University of California Press, 1997), p. 396.

David Wilson expressed the thesis that the pantheistic nature of Germanic religion and its prolonged contact with Christianity made acceptance of a Christian God easy. He points to the burial crosses of Middleton as evidence of the fusion in some form of pagan and Christian tradition and cites with approval Berg's assertion that the "Christian teachers were using certain Norse legends—particularly the legend of Ragnarok—as a means of demonstrating the fall of the pagan gods and the rebirth of the world through Christ's death on the cross and his defeat of the devil."[3] To which I would add, it is not only the fall of the gods at Ragnarok that they were using, but above all, the sculptors of the crosses were using the accompanying story of the tree Yggdrasil and its legend of the salvation of the last man and woman or boy and girl through its protection. Moreover, the artists of the crosses seem to have been aware of a pertinent Germanic burial custom.

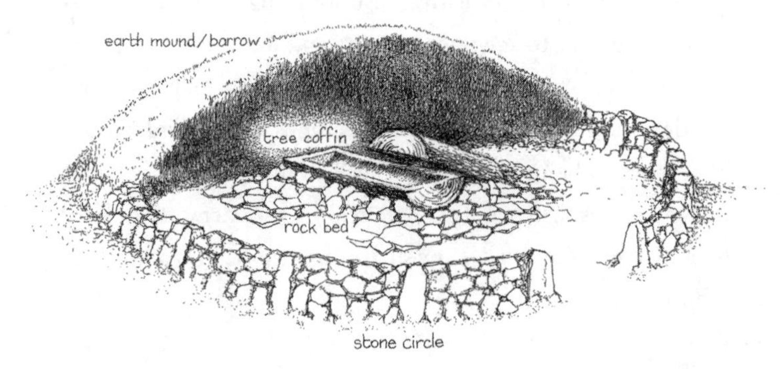

Figure 4.1. The structure of a burial mound centered on a tree trunk coffin. The log rests on stone bedding for drainage and support while the stone circle marks the area and helps prevent erosion of the earth mound. The dead person is enclosed in the hollowed out tree trunk. Late bronze age through the medieval period. Drawing by Laurence Selim.

3. "'The Vikings' relationship with Christianity in northern England," *Journal of the British Archaeological Association*, 30 (1967), p. 46. He refers to K. Berg's article, "The Gosforth Cross" in *Journal of the Warburg and Courtauld Institutes*, XXI (1958), pp. 27–43.

From the bronze age through the Viking period, people were often buried in tree trunks that had been split longitudinally and hollowed out top and bottom to form a coffin (Figure 4.1). In my opinion, as ritual follows myth, this must have been in order to benefit by parallel from the protective tree powers promised in the Yggdrasil legend. In pagan times these tree coffins were often aligned northward, on an axis following that of the World Tree, facing the north star and Woden's Wain which circled it. The lid portion of the coffins that have been discovered often have a long double-headed snake carved on it in such a way that each head of the snake emerges on opposite ends of the coffin. This snake will no doubt be seen by many as serving an apotropaic purpose, serving to repel the grave robber, and perhaps also, and more seriously, to repel the Nidhogg dragon from devouring the corpse. It should also and primarily be seen however as an identity marker. The double-headed snake on the lid serves a parallel purpose to that of the snakes carved onto the upper eaves of the stave church, that of signaling identity: the serpents enable the mourner to see the coffin as the trunk of the protective tree Yggdrasil. It seems that such a tree burial must have offered to men who had died peacefully a long way from the battlefield, far from any chance of Valhalla, a hope of living in the next world; and also it offered to the women who had never been on a battlefield a chance to wait inside the protection of the tree until the new world dawned.

Tree coffins date from the bronze age to the Viking age. They have been unearthed throughout the Germanic world of the north and in fairly large numbers in Denmark, Sweden, Schleswig in Germany, and in England. Especially well-preserved examples were found at Oberflacht in southern Germany (sixth century) and in a barrow at Egtved in Denmark (1370 BC). Interesting for our purposes here are the English tree coffins. Fourteen of them were found at Selby, North Yorkshire, on Church Hill, about 12 miles from York and only about 35 miles from Middleton.

In the graveyard stone crosses, then, at Gosforth and especially Middleton, we can see that the story of Yggdrasil's rescue of mankind was regarded by the sculptors as exemplifying and foretelling that Christ's cross would provide its chieftain's protective and rescuing role for those buried in its ground. The Gosforth sculptor envisioned the lower portion of the shaft as a round tree trunk which, as the eye ascends, is seen to become the square upright of Christ's cross. The sculptor consistently with this idea provides the small crucifixion panel on the large cross with no separate cross of its own—the Yggdrasil of the upright shaft is the wood on which he was crucified.

The Middleton sculptor suggested as well that Woden's holy tree forecasts the place, and foretells the treelike wooden means of ultimate rescue. The branches foretell the arms of the cross; the sacrifice of Woden on the tree and his gift of the runes comes to fulfillment in the sacrifice of Christ on the tree and in Christ's gift of his words and the Eucharist. The chevrons in the ring-halo at the top of the cross suggest the new rising sun forecast by the newly emerging sun which follows Ragnarok. The crucifix may also be designed to shock: there is no Christ on the cross, no biblical scenes. Where the crucified Christ should be, there instead is the dead Christian warrior!

In Matthew's Gospel, 5:17, the question of conversion between religions is addressed by Christ in this way, "I did not come to abolish the law and the prophets [the Old Testament], but to fulfil them." In the *Heliand,* the first part of the same phrase becomes: "I did not come to chop down the old law. . . ."[4] Disapproval of Boniface and his axe-handled approach to the sacred tree at Geismar is more than

4. *Heliand*, pp. 1428–29: *Ni quam ic an thesa uuerald te thiu,/that ic feldi thero forasagano uuord, ac ic siu fullien scal. The Heliand, The Saxon Gospel*, Murphy, trans., p. 49 (Song 17).

hinted at. The *Heliand* is an attempt to describe Jesus as also fulfilling the expectations of the "old law" of the North. In the *Heliand* the cross is described not as being some sort of secular gallows, but rather as the more religiously familiar tree on a mountain, a *bôm an berege.* We should thus not be surprised to see Yggdrasil as the rounded bottom portion of the shaft of the Gosforth cross tapering up into the squared top section, which then becomes Christ's tree, the cross. The image of Vidar tearing apart the jaws of the wolf Fenrir on the same side as Christ dying on the cross, foreshadows Christ who by his death forced open the jaws of death. Siegfried stabbing the serpent from a ditch in the earth, hints at Christ lying in his grave preparing to destroy the final serpent of cosmic death. The Middleton crosses too may be read as Christ depicted saying, "I did not come to abolish Ragnarok, but to fulfill it; I did not come to fell the tree Yggdrasil, but to make its story come true, to rescue mortals."

"This fusion of Christian and pagan images, the so called 'pagan iconography of Christian ideas',[5] would, one can argue, be entirely appropriate for the new Hiberno-Norse elite. . . ." says David Stocker,[6] and I concur. The crosses themselves can be dated to the time of Viking rule in Northumbria, and perhaps especially to the time of Ragnald and the Hiberno-Norse rule of York from c. AD 910 to 953. The Middleton crosses have been fairly well preserved because they were reused in the middle of the following century as part of a new church tower built in approximately the year 1050.

5. Anders Bugge expressed this idea in his impressively illustrated seminal study, *Norwegian Stave Churches,* Ragnar Christophersen, trans. (Oslo: Dreyers Vorlag, 1953). See especially pp. 19, 24, 41–46. See also Ch. 2 above.

6. In Anders Bugge's "Irregularities in the Distribution of Stone Monuments," in *Cultures in Contact, Scandinavian Settlement in England in the Ninth and Tenth Centuries,* Dawn M. Hadley and Julian D. Richards, eds. (Turnhout, Belgium: Brepols, 2000), p. 195. Anders Bugge is one of the first to have seen the portal carvings of the Norwegian stave churches as Christian iconography expressed in Germanic mythological form.

There is one more cross still embedded in the masonry that can just be glimpsed lying sideways as a part of a course of stones in the outside south wall of the tower.

The village of Middleton with its Anglian and Viking church of St. Andrew, lies just outside Pickering in Yorkshire, which is about an hour or so north of York itself, and well within the sphere of influence of York's original Danish and then in the tenth-century its Dublin-Norse Viking occupiers and settlers. This would account for the clear Celtic influence on the overall shape of the crosses, especially the ring around the cross head, and the use of standing crosses in churchyards both as sermons in stone and as memorials to the dead. It is equally clear, however, that the scenes and figures sculpted on these Viking crosses are not in the Celtic tradition of biblical scenes of Old Testament—typological images such as Adam and Eve and the tree, or Cain killing the innocent Abel,[7] the slaughter of the Passover lamb, New Testament, or even monastic images, e.g., of Paul and Antony meeting in the desert of Egypt—but rather they are types from the Norse Germanic religious tradition. For example, there is no image of Christ, either crucified or in glory, nor of the saints, nor of any New Testament scene, on any of the Middleton crosses. And yet they are clearly Christian crosses for the dead. I suggest therefore that it is quite helpful to interpret them in the light of parallel Germanic-Christian religious works of the North, such as the nearly contemporary[8] Thorwald's Ragnarok tablet from Kirk Andreas on the Isle of Man, (see Figure 4.2) and the portals of the later Norwegian and Swedish stave churches.

7. These foreshadowing scenes can be found, for example, in the bottom panel of the west face of the high cross of Murdoch at Monasterboise in Ireland.

8. David M. Wilson gives an estimation of time period for the Manx slabs of approximately 930–1030 AD. "Scandinavian Settlement in the North and West of the British Isles: An Archaeological Point-of-View" in *Transactions of the Royal Historical Society*, 5th series, vol. 26, pp. 95–113.

Figure 4.2. Thorwald's cross slab from Kirk Andreas on the Isle of Man, c. 950 AD, depicts the cross in Celtic outline but with Germanic (Viking) mythology. To the right, Woden with his raven on his shoulder, his spear pointed down at his attacker, is being devoured feet first by Fenrir the wolf at Ragnarok. The snakes below and on the sides of the cross as well as the ring-chain motif on the cross shaft with swastika at its top indicate that the cross is the true protector tree, Yggdrasil. Werner Forman/Art Resource, New York.

This associative procedure helps identify the Germanic-Christian poetry of the crosses by focusing on the iconographic language of the Norse mythology, in which, I maintain, they are written. Failing that, the sculpted images may seem to consist of uninventive, syncretistic juxtapositions—pagan myth or secular hunting scene inscribed on a Christian cross but without a well thought out, typological relationship to the Crucifixion. However, there is such a foreshadowing, Old Testament–to–New Testament, type of relationship present in the sculpted events from Germanic mythology. As Dawn Hadley has written in the same vein, "Other sculptures appear to have drawn parallels between Christian teaching and pagan mythology such as on the Nunburnholme (Yorkshire) cross shaft where a eucharistic image is—following a recarving—accompanied by a depiction of Sigurd drinking the blood of the dragon. . . . Christian teaching was being presented in Scandinavian terms."[9]

There have been several threads of interpretation of the two main Middleton crosses. The oldest, Binns's, is that cross B represents a man as he lies in his grave. The man is obviously a warrior depicted with his helmet, or possibly a leather cap, on his head. He is surrounded by his military grave goods. To the observer's left is his long spear, and to the right, in descending order, is his shield, his sword, and on the bottom, his axe. Across his midsection lies his long knife or scramasax. This depiction on the cross shaft would then be very close to the manner in which he was placed in his wooden coffin and buried below the cross. A second interpretation is that the warrior is depicted as sitting on his chair or throne, the two small pellets above his right and left shoulders being taken for knobs at the top of his throne. This interpretation also hopes thereby to explain the shortness of the arms and legs as an attempt, if clumsy, at foreshortening; but unfortunately this interpretation must cope with the more random pellets on the reverse of the cross and one next to the helmet. It seems to me much more likely that the pellets are filling open space. A third interpretation takes the point of view that both sculptures, cross A and B, are highly

9. See Dawn Hadley's "Lordship in the Danelaw," in *Cultures in Contact, Scandinavian Settlement in England in the Ninth and Tenth Centuries*, p. 117.

secular.[10] In cross A there is simply a hunting scene, and in cross B a warrior on his throne. The difficulty with this latter reading of the crosses is that it really makes no serious attempt to interpret the presence of such scenes within the context of a large stone cross; not to mention the ignoring of the very specific *Sitz im Leben* of the sculptures as memorial stones for the dead erected in a Christian graveyard.

In summary response to the above, I have to first say that the most important element of all is the powerful and robust depiction of the cross B itself, together with its Christian warrior framed within it where one would expect the corpus of Christ and/or scriptural scenes; and so I have to differ with the third interpretation. It simply does not take into account the overwhelming framing function of the cross in the sculpture. The second interpretation, while possible, seems a bit contrived. One need only look up at the shield—there is another pellet to its left, between the peak of the helmet and the shield, with no relationship to a chair. I think they serve as space fillers.[11] Ultimately the interpreter must deal with the overall artistic context of the cross.[12]

My approach is to suggest: first, the overarching importance of the myth of the tree Yggdrasil at Ragnarok as an analogue to the Christian

10. See M. Firby and J. T. Lang, "The Pre-conquest Sculpture at Stonegrave," in *The Yorkshire Archaeological Journal*, 53 (1981), pp. 21–2. The authors comment, "The significance of the stag hunt escapes us today but its presence on tombstones of the Stonegrave kind underlines its funerary references."

11. For further discussion, see James T. Lang, "Some Late Pre-Conquest Crosses in Ryedale, Yorkshire: A Reappraisal," (*Journal of the British Archaeological Association*, vol. 36 [1972]), pp. 17–9.

12. Though Lang, op. cit., rejects the idea that this is a heathen Viking grave, he believes that, "We are still left with a memorial of a local aristocrat who saw himself . . . primarily as a lord and warrior. Despite the great cross head, this reflects a thoroughly secular attitude with an eye on prestige rather than on salvation. . . ."

Figure 4.3. Middleton cross A. The tenth-century image on the cross shaft consists of a man in the upper right with a sax in one hand and a downward pointed spear in the other. Two dogs, or a wolf and a dog, are running on the left side, and down below a deer with head tossed back is nibbling on the frame of the scene. This is often seen as a secular hunting scene, but it is also surmounted by a ringed cross and seems more likely a parallel to Thorwald's cross slab, depicting events of Ragnarok. Copyright Corpus of Anglo-Saxon Stone Sculpture, photographer T. Middlemass.

story of the Crucifixion and salvation;[13] second, Germanic myth is used here specifically in the role which the Old Testament often plays in the New Testament: prediction, foreshadowing, providing an

13. Many researchers have noted the importance of sacred trees in the North. For example, Calvin B. Kendall, "From Sign to Vision: The Ruthwell Cross and *The Dream of the Rood*";

explanation whose function is to express some realization about the meaning of an event.

CROSS A

The cross is a powerful, bulky, celtic-style cross, (see Figure 4.3) but with nongeometrically perfect arms. Even the ring or halo bulges here and there in a more organic type of way, suggesting a living entity. There is also some clumsiness in the manner of grouping the figures in the frame.

The image on the cross shaft shows a man with a downward-pointed spear, possibly aimed at the dog or wolf figure below him and to his right. There is a second doglike animal on his immediate right. Below the man is an antlered stag, not running but facing the side, head thrown back and close to the framing edge of the sculpture. Looking at the church-door scene from Roglösa, and especially Thorwald's stone slab from Kirk Andreas for comparison, one can see that, even if clumsily done, the same familiar figures are present on the shaft: man with downward pointing spear, stag with arched neck, dogs/wolf running loose. This group of figures surely is intended to depict more than a secular hunting scene. The grouping would have suggested discreetly to those who were still at home with the old mythology, the mythic, religious moment when Woden defends himself from the cosmic wolf Fenrir, with Garm loose as well, at Ragnarok. The end of the gods and the old religion. The observer

Inge Milful, "Hymns to the Cross: contexts for the Reception of *Vexilla regis prodeunt*" in *The Place of the Cross in Anglo-Saxon England*, Catherine Karkov, Sarah Larratt Keefer, and Karen Louise Jolly, eds. (The Boydell Press, 2006). The association suggested by many researchers is that of the cross with the tree of life from the Eden story. What I would like to suggest, however, is that it is the overlooked myth of the tree Yggdrasil that is of singular importance for explaining the details of form and interpreting the overall meaning of the early medieval cross in the North.

has to see this scene as being enclosed in the cross, as the sculptor designed it. In other words, the observers seeing the cross are reminded of the story of Ragnarok when the tree Yggdrasil, gnawed by the deer with heads thrown back, trembled as the old world ended, but then opened to offer rescue, as the Eddas tell, to Lif and Lifthrasir.[14]

The sculptor has therefore attempted to show his paralleling of the cross to Yggdrasil by giving the arms of the cross a treelike aspect; they are its "branches." It is no wonder then that the cross is sculpted so organically; it is the true tree of rescue, foreshadowed by the ancient story of Yggdrasil, and serving its parallel function—to protect, to shelter from the end, to guarantee preservation and passage to those whom it encloses—from this time to the next. The depiction of the cross in treelike terms serves to elicit a memory of the story promising rescue. Tree features give the cross an identity in the North: it is revealed to be the real Yggdrasil which saves Lif and Lifthrasir at the end of time. It functions just as the conflation of the cross with the bronze serpent does in the New Testament, rescuing from poisonous snakes, or as the conflation of the Crucified with the sacrificial lamb of God whose blood on the doorpost caused the angel of death to pass over the Israelites and begin the Exodus. The Yggdrasil image gives an identity to the cross and explains its function as rescue from death.

CROSS B

Cross B is even more massive and solid looking than cross A (Figure 4.4). Its image is relatively clear and shows a warrior with

14. It seems unnecessarily modern to read this sculpture in a moral vein as Collingwood did, "the subject of the Hart and Hound (or wolf) is supposed to symbolize the christian in persecution." Cited by R. W. Crossland and R. Hayes in "Bound Dragon Crosses at Middleton, Pickering," *Yorkshire Archaeological Journal*, 38 (1955), p. 453.

Figure 4.4. Middleton cross B. The front of this cross is startling for the modern observer by the absence of an image of the Crucified and the presence instead of a fully armed Viking soldier. Framed within the outline of the cross shaft, he is depicted as he would have lain in his grave beneath it, with his helmet on his head, and his sax or short sword across his belt. Near his right arm is his spear; his left hand rests on his axe; and his long sword is near his left shoulder with his round shield above. Copyright Corpus of Anglo-Saxon Stone Sculpture, photographer T. Middlemass.

helmet (possibly with nosepiece), buried (or perhaps enthroned?) with all his military equipment as grave goods: his helmet on his head; his shield, sword, and axe on his left; and his "ger" or spear on his right side. Across his midsection is his long knife or scramasax in a holster. I agree with Binns; this is probably the exact position in which his grave goods were laid out with him in his casket, possibly at one time directly below this stone. This burial with grave goods, weapons at that, has been interpreted recently by Victoria Thompson in her detailed analysis of cross B as giving moral advice to the observer (or possibly to the dead man?) following Ephesians 6, to take up arms against the devil.[15] "Put on the armor of God, with truth as the belt around your waist, justice as your breastplate. . . . hold faith before you as your shield. . . . take the helmet of salvation and the sword of the spirit. . . ." (Eph. 6: 13–17). This seems at first like a good idea, but I think it does not hold up. Such a reading is too moralizing for a monument to the dead, I believe, doesn't take into consideration the overwhelming role of the cross in the sculpture, and leaves out the Viking axe and sax. Once again there is an attempt to read the monument as if it were written in standard biblical language instead of in Norse Germanic. I think instead it is wise to read the sculpture in a more Germanic way: this is a dead warrior, and the arrangement of the weapons serves to identify him as such, looking to his Chieftain for protection.

This soldier, whether he died on the battlefield or not, whether the Valkyries came for him after the fight, or as seems more likely, if he died of old age in his own home in Middleton, is sculpted as being within the cross-tree Yggdrasil. Like Lif and Lifthrasir, he can expect to live because the tree opened up for him and admitted him to live safely within its trunk. Christ's cross is the tree that will protect and sustain him until time ends and his death period is all over. Then, in accord with what one could see as Germanic myth's predictive foreshadowing of Christian Resurrection by saying Hoddmimir's wood

15. Victoria Thompson, *Dying and Death in Later Anglo-Saxon England* (Woodbridge, Suffolk and Rochester, NY: The Boydell Press, 2004).

will provide protection for human life through Ragnarok and then will open again, he will be released to live again in the next world.

Beowulf and Sutton Hoo may have misled scholars. The discovery of hollowed and longitudinally split tree trunks in Germany in which the dead were enclosed and buried, oriented to the north, shows that some who could not follow the example of the ship or mound burial of wealthy leaders also had a way: they could follow the mythology of entering the tree Yggdrasil. A serpent carved on the lids of these caskets may have been intended to repel corpse robbers or, as mentioned, an even more sinister enemy. Burial in a tree trunk would have reminded mourners of the story and thereby given hope of cosmic protection for the dead until the meadows were green again.

> *Odin said:*
> "Much have I traveled, much have I tried out,
> much have I tested the Powers;
> which among men will live when the famous
> Mighty Winter comes among men?" [Ragnarok]
> *Vafthrudnir said:*
> "Life and Lifthrasir, and they will hide
> in Hoddmimir's wood [Yggdrasil];[16]
> they will have the morning dew for food;
> from them the generations will spring."[17] (*Vafthrudnismal*, 45)

The cross itself is thus shown fulfilling the prophesy of the Yggdrasil story, and is therefore sculpted quite organically, in

16. Hoddmimir's wood ["*holt*"] is generally understood by scholars (Carolyne Larrington, Rudolf Simek, John Lindow, etc.) as a kenning for Yggdrasil. Yggdrasil is associated with (Hodd-) Mimir's well, the name "Hodd-mimir" probably meaning something like "rememberer of the treasure," i.e., awareness of the hidden site of Germanic myth's treasure: the holy place of the fates and the gods at the well under the world tree, Yggdrasil.
17. *The Poetic Edda*, Carolyne Larrington, trans. (Oxford and New York: Oxford University Press, 1996), p. 47.

treelike fashion, with uptilted arms and with its organically drawn ring-halo. The slight separation of the head of the cross from the trunk/shaft, almost gives visible expression to the idea that the capability of the Christian cross is not identical to, but is the culmination of, supersedes, the protection foreshadowed by the Yggdrasil myth. And the tree-cross's power goes beyond that of the myth: Yggdrasil rescues only the last two, Lif and Lifthrasir. Christ's tree-cross rescues everyone who steps inside it, at Borgund and at Urnes, at Olskirke and Nykirke, and including the warrior at Middleton here on the stone shaft. In the continental south, the Christian would be represented by the figures of St. John and the Virgin Mary, and the artist would depict them alongside the cross of Jesus. Being inside his tree-cross to be rescued is how the meaning of salvation came home to Germanic people in the North. The cross became a *mundboro,* a provider of protection. Now the artist must depict: from what?

THE REVERSE SIDE

One of the reasons I traveled to Yorkshire is that I wanted to examine what is on the reverse of these crosses, especially cross B with its solitary guest on the front (Figures 4.5 and 4.6).

In the story of Yggdrasil there is one horrible monster that threatens even it; that is the Nidhogg serpent, the great underground dragon that continually gnaws at its roots, as if trying to annihilate existence itself by felling the Great Tree. (It can be seen in the Roglösa doorway, making its deadly way toward the roots of Yggdrasil.) It is a dragon against which even Yggdrasil has no protection except growth alone as the tree is gradually eroded over time.

Figure 4.5. The reverse side of cross A, depicting the dragon-serpent, the Nidhogg, devourer of corpses and of the roots of the tree of life, as held in bonds by the cross, thus offering no threat to the body of the buried warrior. Copyright Corpus of Anglo-Saxon Stone Sculpture, photographer T. Middlemass.

In Germanic mythology, many of the worst monsters are bound by the gods or by the boundaries of the physical world. Summarizing from the *Voluspa* one could say:

Fenrir was bound by Tir at the price of his hand;
Garm the hound of war was bound, chained in front of the cave;

Figure 4.6. The reverse of cross B, also showing that the dragon-serpent is held bound by the cross of life which is very powerfully sculpted above it. The Nidhogg snake is eyeing the observer, but the sculptor, perhaps remembering the sad fate of Thor at Ragnarok, has carefully threaded the unbreakable bonds right through the poison-delivering openings in the fangs. Copyright Corpus of Anglo-Saxon Stone Sculpture, photographer T. Middlemass.

the serpent Jormungand was bound by the edge of the earth to stay in the sea,
even Loki the trickster was bound by the Æsir to three stone slabs,
all until Ragnarok, the day of doom, should come.

Germanic mythology in its realism acknowledged that the forces of deadly violence, chaos, deceit, and erosion can never be removed from life but they can often be held down by the force of gods and mankind—they can be tied up and bound until Ragnarok. There is one terrifying exception, however: no one, no god, no giant, is ever imagined in Germanic myth as being capable of binding the eater of the dead, the devourer of corpses, the underground serpent, the Nidhogg. He, or it, is the force of death and of ultimate oblivion itself—the one who attempts to bring down the cosmic tree of life. The Nidhogg dragon eats corpses; it is the frightening force, the Anglo-Saxon *wyrm*, that reduces the already dead to nothing.[18]

> The ash of Yggdrasil suffers agony
> more than men will know:
> a deer bites it from above, and it decays at the sides,
> and the Nidhogg rends it beneath.[19] (*Grimnismal*)
> . . . .
> Men tread the road to hell and the sky splits apart [at Ragnarok]
> [Woden is devoured by the Fenris wolf; Thor is killed by the venom of the Jormungand snake]. . . .
> There comes the dark dragon flying,

18. See Victoria Thompson, op. cit., pp. 143–8. This is a good report on the role of the *wyrm*, especially in the plural. Restricting herself to Anglo-Saxon poetry to provide examples of the use of the worm—while interpreting Hiberno-Norse sculpture—however, robs the sculpture of some of its mythic power. The author finds many good examples of the worms, but misses the Nidhogg. She thinks a priest or a biblically minded layman might see cross B's dragon as the dragon-devil from the Book of Revelation (Rev 12:3–4). A biblically minded layman might also well be doubtful that this is the dragon whose tail brings down one third of the stars; but Edda-minded, the identity of the corpse-devouring snake on the reverse of the tree-cross, and its intent, with a corpse in plain view on the front, is sinister and clear.
19. *The Poetic Edda*, Larrington, trans., pp. 56–7.

the shining serpent, up from the Dark-of-moon hills;
Nidhogg flies over the plain, in his wings
he carries corpses. . . .[20] (*Voluspa*)

I looked at the back of the crosses, and there is—and this must have been a shock in the tenth century—a poisonous serpent in bonds. The serpent is tied in the later Jelling style, but the artist has made a special effort to show that his poisonous fangs especially are threaded with unbreakable cord.[21] If you look in the corners, you will see rather poorly drawn legs and feet, or possibly wings.[22] This is no normal serpent, this is the dragon that is a threat both to the Tree and to the corpse of the warrior on the front, the "horrible striker," the Nidhogg. And Christ's cross, alone, is capable of holding the animal bound, protecting both the tree itself, and giving protection to the body of the warrior buried within the tree trunk, the cross. The tree-cross does what none of the Germanic gods ever dared to attempt: it binds the Nidhogg. Even the corpse is protected—a powerful northern way to say that death is completely overcome.[23]

20. *The Poetic Edda,* Larrington, pp. 10–3.
21. James Lang sees a possible association here with Heimdal, "Perhaps the gagging of the dragon is in some way associated with the depiction of Heimdal on the Gosforth Cross where the gaping jaws of two dragons are held at bay by his staff." "Some late Pre-Conquest Crosses," p. 23.
22. The artist forced the dragon's legs into a tight and difficult right angle, a posture necessitated by the rectangular shape of the frame. Curiously, this is same position in which the legs are drawn on the intertwined double dragon on the processional cross from the Staffordshire hoard, which is estimated to be over two hundred years or more earlier. An artistic tradition?
23. The origin of depicting death as bound with cords may lie in the iconography of the Eastern Church. Byzantine icons of the Resurrection often show Christ rising from the dead, holding Adam in one hand and Eve in the other, the gates of hell/sheol smashed beneath him, and on the ground, bound hand and foot, is the dark figure of the master of the underworld—death and/or the devil. Eastern Christian influence may also possibly be found in the clear use of a Greek cross at the top of the shaft of the overall Latin cross at Middleton and in many other of the Hiberno-Norse crosses.

Figure 4.7. The side of cross B, showing the intertwined knot work, which actually consists of just two interlaced loops of cord. Copyright Corpus of Anglo-Saxon Stone Sculpture, photographer T. Middlemass.

THE SIDES

One can imagine a Viking burial in the Middleton churchyard with this very stone standing at the head of the grave. Mourners and friends lower the body into the ground while thoughtfully looking at this cross set at the head of the excavated grave, and then walking around it with reverent attention, taking in the message of the front, the back, and the sides. A person performing this circumambulation would note the front depicting the Germanic warrior protected from death; the back depicting the bound Nidhogg; and the sides exhibiting formidable patterns of interlaced lines. Today we have erosion as a problem with one of the sides of cross B, but the other was protected by being the side not exposed to the weather (Figure 4.7).

This side of cross B has two figure eight loops, one at the top of the shaft and the other at the bottom, united by an extended figure eight knot in the middle. This pattern is found again in simplified form at the end of the cross arm with a figure eight loop held by a circle. The shaft of the cross containing the dead warrior, and the head of the cross with the shining ring of Christ's Resurrection, are shown by the knotted sides of the shaft and cross beam, to be tied together in one fate. Often the sides of standing crosses exhibit intertwining motifs of vine scrolls or rope work whose purpose may seem merely to be a demonstration of the artist's carving ability, but in their quiet way they show the cross shaft and cross head to be organically united, a whole and living tree. The structured knot work of the side of cross B, moreover, may possibly hint to the observer of this cross that the artist was well aware of his interreligious method: cross B speaks of salvation in two religious languages tied together. Physically, the sides of the cross serve to join together the images on the front and back, and here also to intimate the nature of the art of this cross, and thus assist in how to interpret it. The stone monument is composed of the weaving together of the loops of the threads of two stories, Germanic and Christian, concerned about the events of the end and about rescue from death. The carved stone itself joins these two, speaking in sculpted form and mass, a prayer of hope in stone. May the warrior within share the fate of Christ the crucified: may the sunlight of the Resurrection shining in the haloed cross head be bound by intertwined cords to the cross shaft and to the warrior within.

There are poetic elements from two languages present on Mid dleton's cross B, Germanic and Christian, joining to help the stone speak—the warrior, open eyes, weapons, the cosmic tree, the circled cross head, the Viking helmet, the corpse, the corpse-eating dragon of oblivion, the weight of the cross shaft, binding cords, the radiant halo shining around the cross head, all joining to retell the tale of the new and powerful protection offered by Christ the chieftain's raised cross tree . . . as it was foretold long ago by the ancestral tale of Ragnarok, the Nidhogg, and Yggdrasil.

PART II

IN POETRY AND RUNES

Chapter 5

The Trembling Tree of *The Dream of the Rood*

Two of the three versions of *The Dream of the Rood* have it. The longest version, the Vercelli copy, and the shortest, the Brussels Cross with its mere two lines, both have it: the cross tree was "*byfigynde,*" trembling.[1] In a way, this single striking word captures the heart of the poem: the cross is a tree that is alive and aware and is reacting to the Crucifixion. It is awed and frightened by what is about to happen, and overwhelmed by its recognition of the person who is approaching to die on it. This in itself serves immediately to call up echoes of the primeval situation in Germanic mythology when the suffering tree shakes in fear and in awe of what was coming upon the world.

Is there a special Germanic riddle to the identity of the mysterious, trembling, speaking tree, the cross, of this oldest poem in the English language? Scholars have noted the feel of a riddle that exists throughout the poem, almost as if the traditional definitive riddle question were present: "Who am I?" Bruce Dickens and Alan Ross note in their introduction to the text of *The Dream of the Rood* that the poem is composed of two riddle types, the type in which the

1. The Ruthwell cross version expresses the same notion as a prevented acknowledgment: the cross tree had to stand fast, and was not to bow in reverence, despite realizing who was coming to it.

riddle begins with "I see" (Riddle 56—the Cross) and the second type in which "the subject of the enigma is personified and made to recount its own life-history" (Riddle 73—the Spear; Riddle 31—the Cross[?]).[2] Many scholars have derived the identity of the tree of the cross from the Latin hymns of Venantius Fortunatus, *Pange Lingua* and *Vexilla Regis prodeunt,* both of which are related to the arrival of a relic of the true cross at the court of Queen Radegund from the Byzantine Emperor, but in neither of them does the cross tremble or speak. There seems little exploration of the possible Germanic roots of the "I," the *ic* of the central part of the Anglo-Saxon poem, the tree that speaks but also, and significant for identity, trembles.[3] Éamonn Ó Carragáin's magisterial study, *Ritual and the Rood: Liturgical Images and the Old English Poems of the* Dream of the Rood *Tradition,*[4] places great stress on the Romano-Celtic liturgical and sacramental background of the Ruthwell cross and the *Dream of the Rood* poems. But as one of his reviewers complains, Ó Carragáin gives short shrift to Anglo-Saxon, Germanic tradition and allots to it in his study just "a few perfunctory references to *Beowulf.*"[5] The reviewer wishes, as do I, that the more of pre-Christian, religious imagery and ritual of the North had been recognized and seen as integral to his otherwise exhaustive and admirable study of the Rood poem tradition. It is that missing theme that I would like to address here.

2. *The Dream of the Rood,* Bruce Dickens and Alan S. C. Ross, eds. (New York: Appleton-Century Crofts, 1966), pp. 18–19.
3. It might be worthwhile to consider whether or not there might be some influence of Germanic story and myth on Venantius in view of his north Italian birth in a Germanic influenced region.
4. *Ritual and the Rood, Liturgical Images and the Old English Poems of the* Dream of the Rood *Tradition.* British Library Studies in Medieval Culture, Michelle P. Brown and Scot McKendrick, eds. (London and Toronto: The British Library and University of Toronto Press, 2005).
5. Robert Stanton, in *Book Reviews/Religion and the Arts* 12 (2008), pp. 602–29.

Adelheid Thieme's "Gift Giving as a Vital Element of Salvation in the 'Dream of the Rood,'"[6] is a study of Germanic heroic values in the poem, in which she explores the theme of reciprocity. "The principle of reciprocity governing . . . relationships [Father and Son; Christ and his retainer, the cross] inspires the dreamer. He finally comes to realize that the vision of the gold-adorned cross is a gift from God which he is called upon to reciprocate by composing the poem." She concludes that Anglo-Saxon listeners are being instructed in the Christian faith in such a way that, "the Christian faith appears as a set not of alien, but of familiar ideas compatible with the *secular* Anglo-Saxon experience." [italics mine] To this I would only add that, in parallel to the Middleton and Gosforth crosses, the audience is also being presented with images derived from Anglo-Saxon pre-Christian *religious* myth and experience. Thus I believe that the riddle of the cross in the poem hinges on not only the initial double identity of the cross as cross of gold and gems versus cross of wood, but also on the more Germanic double identity of the cross as a non-emotional gallows versus a compassionate and co-suffering tree of rescue. In other words, there is a strong substrate in the poem of the myth of the trembling and long-suffering world tree, Yggdrasil.

THE RUTHWELL CROSS

The Ruthwell cross is generally dated to sometime between the years 700 to 750 AD. It is located in what was once Anglian Northumbria, as are the later Middleton crosses, but on the western side of the country on the north side of the Solway firth, in what

6. In the *South Atlantic Review*, vol. 63, no. 2 (Spring 1998), pp. 108–23.

is now southwest Scotland. The cross was originally erected within the small church at Ruthwell, and, according to Paul Meyvaert's ingenious hypothesis, in parallel to the Plan of St. Gall, stood in the center of the church midway along the east-west axis of the nave.[7] If so, the cross would have been a very impressive pillar in the middle of the small church, reaching up to the roof beams and perhaps also being a central support for them. This in itself would give an "under the tree" form to the interior of the church, one that we have seen in Christianization-era churches such as the central-mast stave churches in Norway and the round churches on Bornholm in Denmark. It is thus highly appropriate that the Ruthwell cross have two sides depicting the intertwined vines and animals symbolic of the northern tree of life, and suggesting again that the cross of Christ around which the congregation and clergy are gathered and under whose branches they are sheltered performs the protective function of Yggdrasil given in the story of Ragnarok.[8]

If we begin with this earliest known version of the poem of the rood, examining it from a Germanic-Christian point of view, different items spring into view. First, the poem is inscribed on the cross in runes. This is not just an alternate writing form to the Roman script which is also present, but the Germanic fuþark, or, in Britain, fuþorc, as we have seen, carries other connotations as well. This

7. *The Ruthwell Cross, Papers from the colloquium sponsored by the Index of Christian Art, Princeton University, 1989*, Brendan Cassidy, ed. (Princeton, NJ: Princeton University Press, 1992), pp. 151–57. See also the diagram on p. 105, Fig. 3, which lays out Meyvaert's reconstruction of the original positions of the topmost stones of the cross. I accept his arrangement and will use it throughout.

8. A similar posture of protection under the cross-as-tree can be seen in the famous twelfth-century ivory cross at the Cloisters in New York, where Adam and Eve are seen seminaked clinging to the bottom of the cross. Adam has his arms completely around the cross shaft, and Eve is reaching up to the sawn off branches of the cross. See Elizabeth C. Parker and Charles T. Little, *The Cloisters Cross, Its Art and Meaning* (New York: The Metropolitan Museum of Art, 1994), p. 51. See also the mid-eleventh-century treelike cross from Flanders, p. 50.

script derives mythically from the experience of Woden, who hung on the tree Yggdrasil for nine days and nights, and then reached down and grasped the runes and made a gift of them to mankind—a gift which as Professor Thieme would say, calls for a reciprocal gift of runes, the carved poem itself. Seeing runes carved on Christ's cross and reading them causes further recollection of the Germanic hanging tree and may serve to suggest that the hanging of Christ is also such a runic gift, especially with the shedding of blood on the wood to achieve human rescue from death. To achieve their magic power, runes were painted with blood, and thus it is not surprising that the overall poem refers to the blood soaking the cross[9] and thereby, so to speak, filling the letters of the poem with magic power, as will be discussed in chapter six, and enabling them, and the cross, to speak. The runes are, as are the people asleep in the poem, speech-bearers.

The position and use of runes on the Ruthwell cross is also telling. Instead of being carved around the biblical and monastic scenes on the panels of the broader front and back sides of the cross shaft, the original east and west sides, the runes are carved on the on the narrower north and south sides (Figure 5.1). The poetic lines are carved almost in the form of a priest's stole, encircling from above and on the two sides the images of life contained within. The poem's very position on the cross highlights the north and south sides' intertwined images of plant and animal life and suggests both the importance of these images for the interpretation of the runic inscription,

9. For a well-considered interpretation of the relationship of the bleeding and sweating of the crucifixion's depiction in the poem, i.e., the role of "moisture" and the drenched state of the cross, to baptism, see Elaine Treharne, "Rebirth in the *Dream of the Rood*" in *The Place of the Cross in Anglo-Saxon England*, Catherine Karkov, Sarah Larratt Keefer, and Karen Louise Jolly, eds. (Rochester, NY: The Boydell Press, 2006), pp. 145–57. Even more impressive might be the thought that Anglo-Saxon converts from Germanic religion, accustomed to hear of the dew as coming from the branches of Yggdrasil, might have felt at home being baptized with water associated with this "tree" as they stood at its foot, looking up, in the middle of the church.

Figure 5.1. The narrower south side of the Ruthwell cross. The inscription at the top reads "Khrist was an. . . ." (Christ was on. . . .) and then descends on the right side to "rodi" (the cross). Copyright Corpus of Anglo-Saxon Stone Sculpture, photographer T. Middlemass.

as well as the inscribed runes' importance for the identification of the animal-filled plant. What is enveloped by the runic lines on these two sides is the growing vine containing the birds and animals of the "inhabited vine scroll." The Ruthwell runes around the vine complex give the magic of human voice to the cross, true, but more specifically, the runes give speech to the vine and its resident animals, the plant in which all living things are the branches, in other words, to Yggdrasil.[10] The Latin *tituli* of the panels of the east and west sides of the cross, on the other hand, do no such thing. They describe the events in the panels. Something parallel but with human emotion is true of the *Vexilla Regis* and the *Pange Lingua.* In the Latin hymns, however, the cross is sung to, but in the Anglo-Saxon *Dream of the Rood* the cross sings. That enormous change may have suggested the appropriateness of the use of two different alphabets on the cross, one for information, the other for the more magical purpose of enabling tree speech. If the fuþark, moreover, contains a veiled allusion to Christ, or to his prayer, of which the sculptor was aware, then runic letters would not necessarily have to be considered entirely pagan. It would be all the more appropriate to carve runes to use as the alphabet in which the words of his cross take the form of human speech. This important possibility of such an allusion is one we will devote our attention to in the following chapter.

Here, the tree on which Christ was crucified was the tree of life, but, not so much the tree of life from the Garden of Eden, of which we have no poetic description and only the briefest mention in Genesis, nor even Eden's tree of the knowledge of good and evil, but rather the magic and rune-bearing cosmic tree of Northern poetry. In Germanic, poetic terms, the Ruthwell cross suggests that Jesus was actually crucified on the wood of the world tree. *Krist was an rodi,* "Christ was on the tree-cross." On this living and, following Tacitus, fruit-bearing, rood, capable of both supplying runes and having feelings, he was performing the rescue of all of creation in fulfillment of what was predicted by the ancestral story of the rescue of Lif and Lifthrasir by the opening up of the tree Yggdrasil when it saved two

10. For more on the story of the "talking twigs" of Yggdrasil and the Norns as possibly present in the sequence of the staves in the fuþark itself, also see Chapter 6.

persons and sheltered them all through the time of the doom of the gods at Ragnarok. It is not surprising that this tree should speak, have feelings, and protest that human beings do not seem to recognize what they are doing, killing the chieftain of all natural life.

A simple but poignant confirmation of this allusion to the story of Yggdrasil can be seen at the very top of the Ruthwell cross, where there is an eagle perched on the topmost branch of the tree. (The eagle parallel to it on the opposite side of the stone has been identified as the eagle of St. John the Evangelist.) The two uses of the eagle, scriptural and Germanic, indicate that the sculptor artist is aware that he is using one symbol in two contexts, and moreover he is speaking bilingually of a double tragedy: the paradox of life being killed on a Tree, and the paradox of nature realizing it (the eagle in the tree) and human beings not.

Because of the tree, and the eagle's perched position above it, I believe this image of the solitary eagle found on the topmost cross arm of the Ruthwell cross has to be that of the great eagle perched on the top of the world tree, Yggdrasil, and the movement of whose wings creates the winds of the earth, and whose eyes, personified as the hawk Veðrfölnir ("stormwind-pale"), see everything. The eagle on the highest branch of the tree is there to confirm the identity of the inhabited vine on the north and south sides as representing "the windy tree," the Awesome One's Horse, and forerunner of the cross as savior and support of all creation. One circuit around the cross reminded the Anglo-Saxon twice that all creation was affected by the death of Christ on the wood. The runic letters of the inscription itself intimate that his Crucifixion was foreshadowed by the story of Woden hanging on the tree and grasping the runes, and that the preservation and resurrection of life that happened through Christ's tree, was foretold by the story of the rescue of the rescue of Lif and Lifthrasir by Mimir's wood.

The panels on the east and west sides of the Ruthwell cross have been the subject of most of the study of the cross. Surprisingly, these panels do not contain scenes of the passion and death, except on the base of the cross, which, it seems, is later, and is in any case highly eroded. Instead of the scenes one might have expected from knowing the apposite section of *The Dream of the Rood*, the east and west faces contain panels that have been interpreted by Paul Meyvaert as grouping around the themes of *Ecclesia* and *Vita Monastica*, or the two forms of life grouped around the tree during Mass in the Ruthwell church: lay Christians and professed monks, and are accompanied by Latin inscriptions.[11] The Ruthwell cross is thus, like the crosses at Middleton and Gosforth, bilingual: the north and south faces speaking in the foreshadowing and evocative language of Germanic myth, and the east and west faces speaking in the language of the Bible and the church—appropriately indicated to the eye of the observer by the artist's using both Anglo-Saxon runes and Roman letters (Figures 5.2a and 5.2b).

There is also some crossover of animal life to human life from the Yggdrasil vine, which can be seen in several images on the east-west panels. The north-south runic sides contain animals dwelling in and living from the tree, as in the Yggdrasil myth; however, the events portrayed on the church and monastic sides also contain scenes that require human companionship and animal life. The "monastic" side of the cross begins at the bottom with the scene of Mary and the child Jesus going into, or returning from, Egypt, with Egypt's desert understood here as the monastic life. The dominant moving figure in the panel, thanks to the near elimination of Joseph on the left, is the hurrying donkey, who like the cross itself of the *Dream* poem

11. *The Ruthwell Cross*, pp. 95–166.

Figures 5.2a and 5.2b. Engraving on two of the sides of the early eighth-century Ruthwell cross. The runic poem is on the right side alongside the vines; in the center on the left side, Christ is shown standing on two animals as lord of living things. The juxtaposition of the two languages and alphabets, Germanic runes on the narrower sides and Latin letters on the broad sides, is in striking harmony with each one's relationship to the particular content it expresses: in runes, Christ's cross is the speaking tree of life/in Roman letters Christ's person is the lord of life. Copyright Corpus of Anglo-Saxon Stone Sculpture, photographer T. Middlemass.

section inscribed on the north and south sides, is, along with Mary, a living bearer of Jesus. The next panel shows Paul and Anthony meeting in the desert, where they broke bread that was brought to them by a raven. Jesus is then seen in the panel above the two hermits, blessing and accepting the reverence of two animals, the "beasts and dragons" that the inscription tells us "recognized him" in the desert.[12] The animals realize who he is.[13]

The next scene in ascending order shows, I believe, the Visitation, with both Mary and Elizabeth pregnant, bearing life, and in which John leapt in the womb in recognition of Jesus.[14] Finally at the top of the cross head itself comes the figure of the eagle, sculpted, as mentioned, not within the vine or branch as the other birds and animals are on both north and south sides, but perched upon it, suggesting the eagle of the World Tree and implying that sight, vision, meditation upon all of this activity of life, is a part of the cross's presentation of, as Meyvaert would say, I. *Ecclesia,* and II. *Vita Monastica.* To this I would add: and III. and IV. *Natura* sive *Arbor Mundi.*

Now we come to the cross head itself. The uppermost cross arm contains the eagle on the fruited branch, as described. The lower cross arm, under the boss, contains the mysterious figure of an archer kneeling with fully drawn bow, about to shoot diagonally upward. This I believe, relates directly to the Christ and the cross being wounded with "arrowheads" in the poem—especially since the archer is taking aim at the middle point of the end of the right-hand arm of the cross, where the hand of the Crucified would be. The presence of an archer panel indicates to me that the sculptor of the Ruthwell cross was aware of the poem's use of arrows for nails, and thus when the archer panel was sculpted, the artist has to have been

12. *Bestiae et dracones cognoverunt in deserto salvatorem mundi,* as restored by Okasha, *The Ruthwell Cross, Papers from the colloquium sponsored by the Index of Christian Art, Princeton University, December 1989,* Brendan Cassidy, ed. (Princeton, NJ: Princeton University Press), p. 75.

13. An old theme from Isaiah (1:2), which we will see again in Ch. 7 and Christmas.

14. Many feel that this panel could also be Martha and her sister Mary, representing the active and the contemplative life. The partially eroded inscription has a "þa" that is taken for part of "Martha," rather than Elizabeth. The mixed runic and Roman letters of the inscription, however, may indicate an unsure carver. The pose is that of Mary and Elizabeth at the visitation, though the remnants of the *titulus* would seem to favor Martha and Mary.

aware of the content of the runic poem and decided to represent the source of the arrow wounds, an archer. There is no indication of nails anywhere; Christ died limb-weary, as the poem explains, the young hero wounded and bleeding from arrows.[15]

The other two figures that would have been on the cross arms seem to have disappeared with the seventeenth-century destruction of the monument itself. They may one day be recovered. My thought would be that the figures for the two missing arms, on this side, would have to be in parallel to the eagle and the archer, that is, from the Germanic tradition. I would not be surprised if they were the two ravens of Mind and Memory.

On the side of the cross with the Crucifixion on the base, Mary is shown at the Annunciation, the moment in which she first becomes the bearer of a new life. The curing of the man born blind who thereafter comes to behold Christ who healed him, is the next panel, a highly significant one, I believe, since it shows a man coming to do what the animals and so many of the panel figures do: recognize who Christ on the rood is—an appeal to the observer. Above this panel, Christ is standing with Mary Magdalene the sinner who also recognized him, like the animals in the desert, and wept over her sins and dried his feet with her hair. The last panel on the shaft is an image of a man holding a lamb. Most scholars feel it must be John the Baptist, who also recognized Christ in the desert and referred his disciples to him by calling him the "Lamb of God."

15. This metonomy of arrowheads for the nails was suggested in *Fragments of History, Rethinking the Ruthwell and Bewcastle Monuments*, Fred Orton and Ian Wood with Clare A. Lees (Manchester: Manchester University Press, 2007), p. 187. The author of the *Heliand* would have been proud. I find the presence of the archer panel on the cross arm, together with arrows for nails in the poem, convincing evidence that, *pace* Meyvaert, the carving of the runic poem on the north-south sides and the program of the panels of the east-west sides of the Ruthwell cross were imagined as parts of a single artwork.

Christ is associated with life itself at Ruthwell and is recognized as such through association with the natural world of animals.[16] Finally at the cross head itself, two of the four evangelists are on the vertical arms: on the upper arm is St. John, accompanied by, and seemingly talking to, his symbol, the eagle. The depiction looks suspiciously like a recollection of Woden getting information from one of his ravens on the c-type bracteates. Beneath the boss, on the lower arm, St. Matthew the evangelist is talking to his symbol, the (winged) human being. This would mean that the missing crossbar should have, on either side of the boss, St. Luke with his winged ox on one of its arms and St. Mark with his winged lion on the other.

The top stone of the cross, the vertical arm of the cross, displays the two themes of the cross in the two eagles: the eagle of the Tree: *visus*; the eagle of St. John: *vita,* and the intertwining of the two in the speech of the saintly human beings who lived and heard and recognized: *verbum.*

Without the runic inscription on the cross, one could be justified in regarding the Ruthwell cross as everywhere being a description of life: human converse, Christ teaching, lambs, vines, birds, small animals feeding and resting in the entwining twigs, the eagle on the fruitful branch, and even the four evangelists talking to their living symbols. The poetic runes of the *Dream,* thus come as a bit of a reminder, a shock or sort of protest, as they do in the Vercelli version, that all of this was gained for individuals at a nonrecognized paradoxical price to the Savior and

16. In Latin, *anima* is, of course, associated with the life or soul of any living being as well as that of a human being. *Animalia,* "animals" thus does not have the same nonrational connotation as *bestiae,* "beasts." This makes even more significant the Latin *titulus* that goes with the panel of Christ and animals that even "*beasts*" and dragons, *cognoverunt,* recognized him in the desert.

his tree.[17] The cross was a wooden and vulnerable tree of life, and the price paid upon it was, of all things, a death, the death of a living God-man. The sculptor who wrote the text around the vine scroll of the tree must have felt the stretch of what he was doing: carving in stone a protest in favor of wood, carving on a stone cross a speech from the original wooden one. Sculpting runes not about the Annunciation but about the suffering and death, with blood running down the wooden branches of one whom he had just called the Iudex Æquitatis, which one might be tempted to translate for its gentle irony, "The Judge of Fairness."

The artist brings the wood of the cross, using the power of ancestral runes that encircle the sculpted Tree with its birds and branches, to human speech:

> Almighty God took off his gear and clothes
> When He wanted to climb onto the gallows,
> Courageous in the sight of all men.
> I did not dare bow,
> I had to stand fast.
> I lifted up the powerful king,
> Heaven's lord. I did not dare bend or bow.
> People mocked the two of us together.
> I was drenched with the blood
> That poured out of this Man's side when he sent off his spirit.
> Christ was on the pole, [the cross];

17. Ó Carragáin sets his focus on a different aspect of the central conflict of the poem. In his eyes the main conflict is not so much an ontological and epistemological paradox as an ethical problem: "that the Cross, loyal to its lord, is required 'by the Lord's word' to destroy its lord's life." *Ritual and the Rood,* p. 7–8. His approach to the plants and animals of the vine scroll is that they indeed represent the tree of life, but he relates their function to the "sun's daily and yearly course," as pointing to the "growing days" for Christ and "lessening days" for John the Baptist (p. 285). The runes, for him, do not relate to the speech of the vine scroll.

Even so, noblemen were hurrying there from far away,
to the One alone. I beheld it all.
I was sorely troubled with sorrows.
To these men I bowed down, to their hands.
Wounded with arrowheads
They laid Him down, weary in limb.
They stood for Him at the head of his corpse;
They beheld there Heaven's Chieftain. And He rested himself
there a while.[18]

A more startlingly emotional contrast to the sobriety of the Latin panel descriptions could scarcely be imagined. Do living people not recognize what was done on the wooden pole for their lives? Yggdrasil recognized him. The animals realized who he was. The eagle above the Tree is looking down, and sees. Perhaps on the other side of the capstone the eagle inspires St. John the Evangelist to tell the story. And so we come to a joint theme that binds the whole sculpture together: recognition, realization. Normally the cure of the man born blind is the one panel that is almost completely ignored in interpreting the Ruthwell cross. I think it may be the vital clue. If you put together the motif of awareness on the part of animal and plant life alongside the need for sight on the part of the man born blind, you are reminded immediately of the prophet Isaiah's forceful, poetic reproach to the people of Israel that they are unaware of their divine master, less perceptive and feeling than their own animals in the stables. We know this passage from Christian use of the ox and the ass in a transferred sense at the Christmas manger:

18. For illustration of the original text on the cross and discussion of the symmetrical structure of the verses with reconstruction and comparison to the Vercelli text, see David Howlett, "Inscriptions and Design," in *The Ruthwell Cross*, esp. pp. 82–93.

> Hear O heavens, and listen, O earth, for the Lord speaks:
> An ox knows its owner,
> and an ass, its master's manger;
> But Israel does not know,
> my people has not understood. (Isaiah 1:2–3)

The poet of the Rood poem tradition has used the tree of the cross as his "Old Testament" prophet. Not the biblical ox and the ass here realize who this is, but the tree with its birds and animals, soaked with the blood and sweat of the brave young warrior, realizes. The tree recognizes its owner and naturally trembles (in the Vercelli version), tries to bow, but has to stand steady. The tree's feelings come out in its sympathy for the suffering Lord of the living, in its enduring of mockery with him, and in its gentle appreciation of those who take him down from the cross—to them the upright cross bows. The cross feels great sorrow, covered with his blood, and the tree remarks with heartfelt compassion that Jesus, limb-weary and become a corpse, finally is given a little while to rest. Like the dumb ox and the ass who at least know their owner, Yggdrasil and its hawk-eyed eagle realize who this is. The Ruthwell cross asks for the healing of human blindness. The figures in the panels recognize him, carry him, even in pregnancy—John the Baptist leaped in the womb—the animals in the vine scroll and on the panels go further: they recognize the irony of the giver of *anima* being killed. The tree Yggdrasil, speaking in runes cut from its branches carved on the cross, acts for all nature in accord with Mary Magdalene when it says, in the Vercelli version, *weop eal gesceaft*, all of creation wept.[19] Recognizing him even when wounded and limb-weary, exhausted

19. The mysterious runic fragment on the upper stone of the Ruthwell cross, *dægisgæf*, has been ingeniously interpreted by Swanton as [*wæp*]*dæ giscæf*[*t*], "creation wept." *The Dream of the Rood*, M. Swanton, ed. (Exeter, 1987), pp. 47–48.

to death, the tree-cross asks the devout observer contemplating all four sides of this cross, all creation wept, do you?

The Vercelli version of *The Dream of the Rood* was written down approximately two centuries later, about the year 950 AD, and is thus roughly contemporary with the Middleton crosses. Though the exact relationship between the two versions of the *Rood* poem, though often very close, is not altogether clear, it is very clear that they are related and may perhaps both go back to an common older source, oral and/or written. This means for me that the poem's central conceit of the talking cross was a persistently popular one in the world of early English Christian devotion.

There is also a very brief, third version going back to the eleventh century to an inscription on the Brussels cross which consists of two lines, probably written by a Wessex copyist, the second of which sounds the highly distinctive note that links the Rood tradition to that of Yggdrasil:

> Rod is min nama, geo ic ricne Cyning
> Bær *byfigynde* blode bistemed.
> (Cross is my name; long ago,
> *trembling*, drenched in blood, I bore a powerful king.)[20] [Italics mine]

ÓCarragáin has a beautiful reconstruction of the use of this processional cross on a great feast day:

> As the cross was borne, at the head of a procession of clergy, up the nave towards the altar area, the congregation waiting to worship the relic first saw the jeweled front of the cross, which

20. Ó Carragáin, *Ritual and the Rood*, pp. 7–8.

> recalled the glorious wounds of the Passion. Meanwhile the clergy, advancing in procession behind the reliquary, could see the glorified Agnus Dei, surrounded by the evangelist-beasts. For them, the act of solemn procession was an image of the Church's pilgrimage. . . . As the cross was borne past members of the congregation, (such as monks waiting in their choir-stalls) the jeweled front, with its recollection of Christ's victory on Good Friday, suddenly gave way to the glinting gilded silver of the back, with its tableau of the parousia. The two broad faces of the faces of the cross presented in sequence two aspects of a single vision."[21]

As the cross moved forward above the heads of the congregation, no sign of trembling would have been present, just the shimmering of gems, the "glorious" wounds of Good Friday. There is surely no sign of bleeding. The poet of the *Dream* in his vision saw through the processional cross's gold and silver cover to recognize the wood of the original, dripping blood. There is no riddle to the identity of the golden processional cross, but the identity of the wood underneath its golden sheathing invites thought.

Let turn to look at the role of the tree in *The Dream of the Rood* poem as found in the Vercelli version. Richard North has made an impressive argument for the identification of the speaking Tree in the poem as Yggdrasil. In his *Heathen Gods in Old English Literature*[22] he argues that seeing the World Tree as Woden's Horse, Ygg-drasil, ("Ygg" awesome one + drasil, "horse," "mount"),[23] explains nicely

21. *Ritual and the Rood,* p. 344.

22. In the series *Cambridge Studies in Anglo-Saxon England* 22 (Cambridge: Cambridge University Press, 1997), pp. 273–303.

23. The identification of Woden's horse, Sleipner, with the tree Yggdrasil, and its cosmic manifestation in Woden's Wain (*Ursa Major*, the Big Dipper), can also be found everywhere on the Danish c-bracteates of the time of the barbarian invasions (*Völkerwanderungszeit*).

the enigma of the cross at the end of the poem promising to come "fetch" the dreamer, calling up old images of the souls of the dead, the *einherjar*, riding on horseback into heaven-asgard. North sees this as according with Christ "mounting" the cross, a close correspondence with Woden's "riding" Yggdrasil for nine nights during his hanging. He further suggests that the gold and jewels covering the cross can be seen as the reward a lord should bestow on a loyal thegn. Finally he associates the emphasis on bleeding as an echo of the death of Baldr, who was killed by his blind brother at Loki's instigation with a mistletoe spear. Baldr then went to hel, the land of the dead, from which he could not be released unless all creation wept. Loki, of course, refused to weep for Baldr, and thus he was never released from the dead. This would give special poignancy to the line of the poem that, at the sight of Christ's death on the tree, "all creation wept" *weop eal gesceaft* (55), foretelling a successful return from hel in view of universal compassion.

The dynamic progress of *The Dream of the Rood* can be divided into three movements or parts. The first part, ll. 1–27, deals with the questioning relationship of the "dreamer" to the cross, with bewilderment on the dreamer's part, as he looks at the double aspect of the cross. In the second part, ll. 28–121, the dreamer progresses from looking to listening, as the cross speaks to him and tells him the story in which the tree played a vital and mortal part. In the third part, ll. 122–155, the "dreamer" comes to the emotional realization that the tree and its feelings must be in him, and come to speak through him, and this brings the reader back to the first line of the poem, "I want to tell. . . ." Structurally, the Vercelli version of the poem needs the interpretive framework of parts I and III to contextualize the words of the cross in part II . The carved runic version of the Ruthwell cross can rely on the stone cross itself and the images of the four sides to serve as an interpretive framework for the cross's speech. The written poetic world of the Vercelli version, on the other hand, requires that verbal descriptions of the golden cross and the internalized cross be expressed in the framework, parts I and III.

The three parts enable a progression that is at the heart of the movement of the poem. In part I, the riddling bewilderment of the dreamer is caused by the changing aspect of the cross that he envisions in the middle of the night when other speech-bearers are sound asleep. He sees in his "best of dreams"[24] the "brightest of trees"; it is covered with gold with its fair gems extending "to the corners of the earth, *æt foldan sceatum*" (8). Later we learn that this shining symbol wound round with light is beheld by everyone, holy spirits on high, men on earth and all this great creation (11–12). The dimensions of the tree, the implication that it encompasses the worlds, reaching over the whole surface of Middlegard, as well rising to the upper world of the holy spirits, certainly sounds like a description using the world tree as its basis. There is even the curious line that everyone beheld it there like an "angel of the Lord," describing the tree as beautiful, fair, because of its being fore-created, *þurh forðgesceaft,* for this. If this is the world tree as it certainly seems, then it is beautiful because it was predestined to be the means of Christ battling death, and becoming the tree of victory, the *sigebeam*.

The night-visionary sees through all the gold and gems that cover the gleaming cross. He says, moreover, that he could make out under all the glorious golden trappings that the gem-covered cross was bleeding on the right side. Now he becomes troubled and bewildered; sometimes the cross appears gloriously covered with precious metal, sometimes it appears dripping with blood and

24. This is a Germanic formula for gnomic riddles such as those in Old English and in the Grimnismal. They follow the style of "Sleipnir is the best of horses, Fenrir of wolves, Yggdrasil is the noblest of trees, Garm is the best of dogs, etc." There are many of these in the poem, the superlatives used of the cross, making the rood seem a native item of Germanic lore.

sweat. And so he wonders and worries. But he treats the mysterious tree of glory and suffering as a puzzlement—a rotating object to be figured out, a worrisome ambiguity to be resolved. Like Sophocles' Oedipus of a thousand years before, who could solve the sphinx's riddle about mankind in a second, but was not so deft about the riddle of himself. This is a stance into which at this point the poet has also steered the reader. The dreamer is underway though, the beauty of the tree reminds him that he is stained with sins, and he uses the lovely and anticipatory word "wounded" to refer to his sinful condition, *forwundad mid wommum* (14).

Then, in part II., the midnight seer of visions begins hearing. "I heard" *ic gehyrde* (26) that the tree was speaking, the best of trees, *wudu selesta* (27), began to speak words. The author loses no opportunity again and again to emphasize that the cross is and was a tree, and we should not miss the point at the transition to part II, that no matter how impressive it was in gold and silver, the cross of Christianity did not "speak" to the Anglo-Saxons until they realized that it was a tree. So it is no surprise then that the tree begins by telling its own story as a real tree cut down at the edge of the forest, cut off from the base of its tree trunk. This is not only to distinguish it from its gold overlay, but to express that it is a natural living thing, and as such, is capable of having feelings and expressing them in voice. The tree expresses resentment at being cut down to be used as a gallows for criminals, it then feels awe as Christ approaches, it attempts to bow down in reverence, it feels aggressively defensive of its Lord and wishes, like a good thane, to crush his enemies—and the tree has enough pride in itself to feel it could crush them all, but feels it must be obedient. And finally when Christ climbs up on the tree to die on it, and embraces the tree with his arms outstretched, the tree trembles.

Without using any words, the tree is eloquent in its trembling. It is following the trembling of the earth.

I saw then the Savior of mankind
hurrying with great zeal when he wanted to climb up on me
I did not dare, against the Lord's word,
bend or break, when I saw the ends of the earth
trembling (*bifian*). I could have felled
all of those enemies, but I stood fast.
The young Hero took off his gear and clothes—that was almighty
God—
strong and determined. He climbed up on the gallows,
courageous in the sight of the crowd, when he wanted to release
mankind.
I trembled (*bifode ic*) when the Man embraced me. However I
dared not bow to the ground,
Nor fall to the earth's surface, I was to stand fast. (33–43)

The first mention of "trembling" above refers to the surface of the earth and can, of course, be referred back to the earthquake mentioned in the New Testament at the time of Jesus's death on the cross: "And when Jesus had cried out again in a loud voice, he gave up his spirit. At that moment the curtain of the temple was torn in two from top to bottom. The earth shook, and the rocks split."[25] When trembling is mentioned again, as Christ touches the tree and the tree trembles, that is another story. It is not to be found in any of the gospels, and is a creation of the poet,[26] a creation that calls to

25. Matthew 27: 50–1. The tearing in two of the curtain of the temple is very important for the Jewish aspect of Matthew's Gospel, but in the Germanic and natural world of the poem, the earthquake is more telling.

26. For discussion see Michael Swanton, ed., *The Dream of the Rood* (Exeter: University of Exeter, 1987), pp. 118–19, 123. The curious suggestion that the trembling of the tree was borrowed from Ephraem Syrus' description of the pillar of Christ's scourging as shaking, or from the Roman standards bowing [not shaking] in the apocryphal *Gesta Pilati,* seems unnecessarily determined to maintain Mediterranean sources, no matter from how far they are fetched.

mind the other tree that trembles on the Day of the Doom of the gods, Ragnarok: Yggdrasil. In the Voluspá we read:

> *Ymr aldit tré, en jötunn losnar*
> *skelfr Yggdrasils askr standandi* (47)
> The ancient Tree groans, the giant [Fenrir] is loose,—
> Yggdrasil's ash trembles as it stands.[27]

If Yggdrasil is the tree that Christ is embracing, then two religions have met. The same Christianity that insists on Saxon rejection of Woden, Thor, Frey, and Saxnot prior to baptism, finds it possible to accept and to embrace Yggdrasil, the World Tree—the concept that the natural world is upheld by a provident and caring protector, a Tree of Life, that feels and feeds life, and suffers death as a loss along with all. And, as the foreshadowing tree of the old religion is embraced by its creator before his death, it trembles.

> *Bifode ic þa me se beorn ymbclypte* (42)
> I trembled as the Man embraced me.

It is no wonder that the poet of the *Dream of the Rood* composed his great work with such beautiful interlacing, as beautiful as that on the crosses at Ruthwell, Bewcastle, and Gosforth. It is not surprising then that enemies mock both the tree and the man together, the dark arrowheads that nail the Savior's hands and feet do so by penetrating deeply into the wood of the rood. Both Jesus and Yggdrasil have to be wounded by the same dark shafts by the same archer in order for him to die and to be held by the tree. Both religions suffer,

27. *The Elder or Poetic Edda, Commonly Known as Saemund's Edda,* Olive Bray, ed. and trans. (London: The Viking Club, 1908), p. 292.

together. When he dies, the blood of wound in the side drenches the cross, in a kind of horrifying baptism, and dark shadows suddenly cover the earth and the cooling corpse. And, together with Yggdrasil who stands for them all,

> *weop eal gesceaft* (55)

"All creation wept," as the corpse of the exhausted and limb-weary warrior is laid down to rest himself a while from the terrible battle. After the cross describes the burial of Christ by his friends, it explains that it too was cut down and buried and, like Christ, was later raised again and then it was covered with gold and silver and exalted under heaven, as the dreamer knows from his first vision.

The pagan tree that was once reviled, by missionaries and by English bishops, is now bragging of the abilities that it now has—abilities, of course forshadowed in the saving role of Yggdrasil in the Edda, but now granted to it by Christ the Savior himself.

Ic hælan mæg, I can save! The tree can save all those who reverence it, the tree that once as a gallows inflicted the hardest of punishments and was hated

> *ærþan ic him lifes weg*
> *rihtne gerymde reordberendum* (88–89)
> Until I opened up the real way to life
> for them, the bearers of speech.

Yggdrasil, as the cross in Christianity, is still performing its old pagan service of saving Life and Lifthrasir, and still doing it by opening a space for them, the bearers of speech. The trembling tree has within it the bifrost, the very rainbow or milky way bridge that the Edda sing of as ("bif-") "trembling, shimmering," and as being the road from Midgard to Asgard/heaven. No wonder then that the tree even claims to have been honored over all the trees on the hillside, honored as much as the Virgin Mary is honored over all of womankind. The comparison is apt, both carried Christ.

After the cross, Yggdrasil, tells the dreamer to tell everyone what he has seen, comes, in Germanic terms, the most amazing inversion of the tradition. The rood tells first of the Christian doomsday, the last judgment, and what Christ's question in front of all the multitude will be: Is there anyone who in the Lord's name would be willing to die on the tree as he did? Every one of the souls begins to be afraid, and though they are speech-bearers, they can't think what to say. Yggdrasil tells them that no one need be afraid:

> *þe him ær in breostum bereð beacna selest*
> *ac ðurh ða rode sceal rice gesecan*
> *of eorðwege æghwylc sawl,*
> *seo þe mid wealdende wunian þenceð.* (118–121).
> who beforehand bears in his breast the best of trees.
> Rather, through the tree, each soul shall arrive at the kingdom—
> [each soul] that, leaving earth-paths,
> intends to dwell with the Ruler.

These are the concluding words of the cross in the poem. The Germanic tradition has been reversed. Salvation does not come by entering the tree Yggdrasil for its protection against the horrors of death at Ragnarok, salvation comes from having the tree Yggdrasil enter into the person, remaining inside the heart during one's lifetime. With the trembling tree in the heart, comes the shimmering rainbow bridge. This is a beautiful transformation of the image of the tree/cross from being an external "mund," an exterior protection into which one can flee, to the image of having the feelings of the rood within, an internal protection. It is simultaneously a call to have the feelings, to have the reverence and thanelike loyalty that the tree had when Jesus climbed up on it, and it trembled. One is saved by having the tree's feelings in one's self. The dreamer's golden and bleeding tree is not a dual-aspect object, not an interesting riddle to be solved, it is something that works when taken into one's self, carried *in breostum.*

Was this insight suggested by liturgical practice? I think there is a possibility that the one ritual practice that seems hithertofore to have been neglected in the study of the poem is the humble "sign of the cross." This cross is indeed not carried before a procession of monks and clergy, but is traced on the body of the individual, initially at baptism, and on the forehead. From the third and fourth centuries the small sign of the cross was made on the breast as well as the forehead. During the time of the monophysite controversy (c. 430 to 553 AD) the sign of the cross appears to have been extended on the body to its full current form.[28] The cross is traced with the right hand over the breast, touching the forehead first, then descending to the heart, to form the vertical rod of the cross, and then from side to side across the *eaxlegespanne,* from shoulder to shoulder, marking the crossbar on the person. This humble gesture, both personal and ancient, made with the hand, an external cross but spiritually internal, may have been in the poet's mind, especially since part III of the poem now begins with the dreamer's prayer to the cross with a happy mind (122).

28. Herbert Thurston, "Sign of the Cross" in *The Catholic Encyclopedia,* vol. XIII (New York: Appleton, 1912), pp. 785–789. Since the sign of the cross is made on the individual to proclaim a state of ownership by Christ and his cross, and to initiate a moment of prayer and rumination within that relationship, it is the perfect introduction to the prayerful nature of the third part of *The Dream of the Rood.*

In part III, the dreamer goes from seeing in part I, and hearing in part II, to feeling and speaking in prayer. In a quite touching manner he complains that he now has few friends left alive, and hopes that the tree's protection will bring him from this passing life *þysson lænan life* to

þær is blis mycel
dream on heofonum þær is dryhtnes folc
geseted to symle þær is singal blis (139–41)
where there is tremendous happiness,
the joy of heaven. To where the Lord's men are
seated at the banquet, to where there is continual bliss.

With the emotions of the trembling rood in his breast as it was embraced, he makes a simple and personal petition:

Si me dryhten freond (144)
May the Lord be my friend.

He who complains of being alone, he now has few friends left in this transitory lifetime, asks his chieftain to be his friend and protector, and through the rood to bring him to the heavenly banquet—an image of happiness shared by both biblical and Germanic tradition, in *Beowulf* and in Luke 13:15ff.

Most moving to me is the second part of the dreamer's prayer, in which he stops asking for admission to the bliss of heaven, and reverts to his earlier contemplative status, this time however with feelings of pride. The ending of the poem is the harrowing of hell, which the poet envisions in military style. He thanks the Lord for giving us a heavenly home, and for using his death to descend to where there were souls burning in fire. He frees them with a victory over Hel, succeeding by death where Woden failed Baldr, and where Yggdrasil could do no more, and then leads his people out of captivity, a troop of souls heading into God's kingdom. The author takes great delight, his own I presume, in imagining the welcome received by this victorious warrior who gives mankind a heavenly home, when he fought his way past the arrow wounds into hel, to give even the dead a heavenly home. The poet imagines in his heart the delight of the angels, and strikes a note of feeling personal pride in the victorious achievement of the fighting leader whom he wants to be his friend. When they see Christ coming back with his forces freed from death, those who were already in heaven take pride in him. In Elaine Treharne's translation:

> The Son was victorious in that undertaking,
> powerful and successful, when he came with the multitudes,
> a troop of souls, into God's kingdom,
> the one Ruler almighty, to the delight of the angels
> and all the saints who were in heaven before,
> who dwelled in glory, when their Ruler came,
> almighty God, to where his native land was.[29] *þær his eðel wæs*

And so the poem ends with a very old and common Germanic word, a word that may even be the end-word of the fuþark, and here used for heaven, *edel*, "the family homestead." He eschews the more cosmic, celestial, and mythic for the more local and familiar, a sure sign that the poem of the rood touched its own author, and that the author touched his Saxon readers. He has brought the cross home—a sign, a beacon, of what his task was all along. The rood-tree, Yggdrasil, is now not an older object, but a part of the heart's

29. http://www.apocalyptic-theories.com/literature/dor/oeodorb1.html.

"forth-creation," expressing itself in reverent trembling, in nature, and in the speech of its carved talking runes, a gentle friend, showing the way to the shimmering bridge-path to heaven.

In the next chapter we will take a closer look at the significance of the fuþark sequence of the speech-enabling runes which in the *Dream* appropriately gave a voice to the tree.

Chapter 6

Yggdrasil and the Sequence of the Runes in the Elder Fuþark

Fascination with the poetic use of runes carved on the Ruthwell cross in the early eighth century as staves that can talk, "bearers of speech," to enable the normally silent cross to raise its voice in speech, naturally leads to curiosity about them and their unique alphabet. For over a hundred and fifty years or more scholars have attempted to interpret the meaning of various runic inscriptions on wood, horn, metal, and stone. Just as in the case of the stave church and the interpretation of the tree shape and the serpents on the roof, interpretation has been impeded, I believe, by an appeal to an unnecessarily restricted, literal, and nonmythological notion of religious magic. As the renowned English runologist, R. I. Page, advised in the conclusion of his *Introduction to English Runes,* the scholar must avoid the further restriction of the library and the study, and "go outside to meet archaeologists, numismatists, art historians, craftsmen. . . ."[1] This good advice will bring us in the present chapter to the examination of gold medallions.

1. Raymond I. Page, *Introduction to English Runes*. Woodbridge, Suffolk/Rochester, NY: The Boydell Press, 1999, p. 232. Professor Page was also renowned for his distinct preference for sober, nonmythical approaches to the meaning of runes, once referring to Professor Tolkien's literary use of runes as "whimsical travesties" (p. 227).

One of the important places where the fuþark is first found is on c-type bracteates from the fifth to eighth century AD, the period of the migrations of Germanic tribes.[2] A bracteate is a small gold disk, stamped with an image and runes on one side, with a small tube at the top so it can be worn as a medal.[3] The c-type constitutes almost half of the number found and has an unusual iconography with Woden on his horse, with birds whispering in his ear and occasionally trailing the whole fuþark behind them. Occasionally there are also birds perched as well on the "limbs" of the "horse," making it suspiciously treelike. The most dominant view is, as with the stave church, that these images have primarily a magic purpose—in the case of the bracteates, not apotropaic, but rather that of healing. Thinking of the Merseburg charms, the bracteates are read as Woden curing a horse. I believe, however, that just as in the case of the stave church's serpents, the image of Woden riding his horse is there to give identity. It is Yggdrasil in kenning form, and identifies the wearer of the medal, like Woden, as one capable of understanding the runes of the fuþark. Before exploring the bracteates, however, it is necessary to attempt to interpret the fuþark itself.

This is a task made quite difficult by the lack of textual evidence of any length, except perhaps in the *Dream*, and thus, understandably, the effort has been attended with varying degrees of success. Even more tantalizingly resistant to interpretation than the second to the eighth century runic inscriptions has been the elder fuþark itself. Just why, in a writing system whose letters have shapes that seem highly indebted to the letters of the Greco-Roman-Etruscan

2. One of those migrations of peoples (also once called "barbarian invasions" by historians) was, of course, that of the Angles, Saxons, and Jutes to England around 450 AD, bringing the runes which would subsequently be used so well at Ruthwell.
3. For discussion of the distribution of bracteates, see Rudolf Simek, *Dictionary of Northern Mythology* (Cambridge: D. S. Brewer, 1993), pp. 43–4.

alphabet, is the sequence of its letters so different from them? The Semitic sequence *aleph, bet, gimel,* and *daleth,* led to the Greek sequence, *alpha, beta, gamma,* and *delta,* as Greeks borrowed and modified Phoenician letters while still retaining as appropriate the sequential order in which they found them. The Romans in turn borrowed and modified their letters from the Greeks but still retained with modifications the basic inherited sequence: a, b, c (= g, k), d. Even our Roman word "alpha-bet" comes from the order of the names of the first two Phoenician-Greek-Roman letters. The equivalent Germanic "alphabet," however, is not an "alpha-beta" but rather a *f.u.þ.a.r.k,* based on its first six letters—a sequence which I would like to suggest is neither random nor borrowed/modified from another system, but a readable entity with two possible interpretations, rooted in the Germanic myth of the nature of the runes as staves seized by Woden as he hung from the tree Yggdrasil. Myths are expressed in words, rather than letters, and my hypothesis is that words, rather than letters, should be sought in the sequence to decipher the fuþark. In my attempt to interpret it, I treat it as a line of mythic poetry whose alphabetical nature rules that each letter of the twenty-four can be used only once.

There must have been some significance behind the deviation from simply following the Greco-Roman alphabetic order of the letters—something leading to the creation of a whole new sequence. The Mediterranean alphabetic sequence is simply inherited from the Middle East and as such has no internal meaning that should be expected; it consists of no words. Is it possible that the deliberately restructured Germanic sequence does spell out something in the rune-row of the fuþark, and could the message be recovered? This is the question to which I would like to offer a possible solution. My method is to use a word-based analysis of the fuþark rather than a letter analysis alone; to accept the myth of Woden and Yggdrasil as helpful in interpreting content and context; and to examine carefully the mythic depiction of the fuþark on several of the oldest preserved artifacts, the Kylver stone of approximately AD 400, and the Vadstena bracteate of about AD 500, together with the depiction on several of the more newly found Danish c-type bracteates from Roskilde. While proof of this hypothesis may not be possible, I think the poetic images on the c-type bracteates and on the stone can be explained by it.

One of the earliest attempts to interpret the fuþark was made by Walter W. Skeat in 1890 when he wrote to *The Academy* from Cambridge.[4] In a letter entitled "The order of letters in the runic 'fu**þ**ork,'" he unleashed an academic battle which, on the basis of the unpleasant replies the journal promptly received, it seems he lost. Skeat's suggestion with regard to the purpose of the rune sequence was: "to give the letters the value of a charm, for the purpose of driving away evil spirits, curing toothache, and the like." His inspiration was that the order and function of the magically potent and quite violent individual runes of the Paternoster in the *Dialogues of Solomon and Saturn*[5] were the backbone of the sequence. Ignoring any possible analysis of the fuþorc as full words, he treats each rune in sequence as an encoded initial letter of a word in a Saxon version of the Lord's Prayer. Thus, according to his reading, it is the Paternoster in Saxon runes which is responsible for creating the Anglo-Saxon fuþorc's sequence.

The first line almost works, for a while: "Our father who art in heaven:" *Father ure, þu in heofon,* F-father, U-ure, Þ-thou, A-an,

4. *The Academy, A Weekly Review of Literature, Science, and Art,* vol. 38, no. 968 [Nov. 22, 1890] (London: J. Murray, November, 1890), p. 477.

5. See my Appendix 3 in *The Heliand, The Saxon Gospel,* esp. pp. 215 ff. The ᚱ rune of the Paternoster is particularly forceful, whirling evil, ghostly opponents around by the hair and breaking their legs on rocks, while the ᛏ rune stabs them in the tongue.

H [?]-heofon. The trouble begins. There is no Saxon word with an initial "r" in the Saxon Lord's prayer for the "r" in the fuþorc.[6] Then, the phrase "hallowed be thy name:" *halgod si nama thin* has to be slightly dislocated. The two words *halgod si* have to be joined as one word so that the h and n will follow each other without an s intervening. The þ of *thin* has to be omitted, the k of fuþork has to be postponed to the *cuman* of "thy kingdom come," and so forth, so that what started out in the first line as an interesting and, if true, easily demonstrated hypothesis, falls apart as a promising but procrustean imposition. Skeat had to manipulate the whole prayer to get its initial Saxon letters to correspond to the rune sequence in the fuþorc. Alas, he saw nothing wrong, he wrote patriotically, with the idea that the inventor of the rune sequence should be an Englishman.

His opponents were not amused. And from that day forward I have not found any scholars who have ventured into the realm of a Germanic, or pagan-Christian reading of the rune-row. Some like Klaus Düwel do admit the importance of the realm of the religious in dealing with the fuþark, but also write that they feel it is dangerous (in the scholarly sense) to do so. After Skeat's effort, this is understandable. It must be admitted it is not entirely good to be fully deterred when another's effort fails, especially if there was some suggestive merit in the approach, for example, if one sees "father" not as useful for identifying the first rune of the fuþark, but perhaps the first word.

6. In 1919 Kluge saw Skeat's 1890 article, and at first is so impressed with Skeat's insight that he thinks up a way to get an "r" into the first line of the Saxon Paternoster. Instead of using "heofon" for heaven he suggests using the Saxon "radur." The fuþork has its necessary "r." Kluge then goes on to deplore the poor execution of the whole idea by Skeat, except for supporting the idea that the beginnings of the Runenschrift are so connected to belief and superstition that one must assume religious underpinnings. "Runenschrift und Christentum," in *Germania: Korrespondenzblatt der Römisch-Germanischen Kommission des Kaiserlichen Archäologischen Instituts* (Frankfurt: Jos. Baer & Co, 1919), pp. 43–48.

In subsequent times the debate has swung back and forth in the context of two other issues: the question of origin, and the question of use, of the runes themselves. Were the runes Greek or Latin in origin, and if Greek, eastern or western;[7] if Latin,[8] were the runes transmitted through Celtic[9] or ogham association, or mainly through north Etruscan letter shapes? Were the runes created primarily for magico-religious or for secular writing purposes? These questions have not been resolved and thus the lively debate continues. Recently there have been attempts to posit the sequence as related to pairings in the alphabets that then by mathematical transformations produce the fuþark.[10] The results, unfortunately, have been summed up recently by Sean Nowak, "In the research there have been attempts made to deduce the sequence of the runes in the fuþark from the sequence in the alphabet, but up to now they have

7. Heiner Eichner discusses the Greek, East or West, theory. Using the g-rune as evidence argues that a "blue" (Eastern Greek) *chi* could have made its way through commerce into a "red" (Western Greek) area. He favors the north Italian area as the place of origin, Adria, Spina, or Venice.

8. Murray Dahm has recently suggested, against Ludwig Wimmer, that Latin cursive, not epigraphic capitals, is at the origin of the rune forms, especially for the p-rune, and that Germanic tribesmen returning from imperial military service brought these Roman letter forms home with them. "Re-examining Latin Cursive Elements in Fuþark Development," in *Amsterdamer Beiträge zur älteren Germanistik*, 55 (2002), 15–21.

9. Bernard Mees gives a fine summary of the origin theories, and concludes that the Celts were the transmitters through Celtic epigraphy and notes a common "mystical association of wood and letters." "The Celts and the Origin of Runic Script," in *Studia Neophilologica* 71 (1999), pp. 144–55. In 2000, he strongly supported a north Etruscan origin and the theory that the runes in the fuþark are grouped in pairs as an aid to memory, in *Arkiv för nordisk filologi*, pp. 33–82.

10. Elmar Seebold, "Fuþark, Beith-Luis-Nion, He-Lamedh, Abğad und Alphabet. Über die Systematik der Zeichenaufzählung bei Buchstaben-Schriften" in *Sprachen und Schriften des antiken Mittelmeerraums, Festschrift für Jürgen Untermann.*, Frank Heidermanns et al., ed. (Innsbruck, 1993), pp. 411–44. Seebold also presented his argument for geomancy and basic pairs in "Was haben die Germanen mit den Runen gemacht" in *Germanic Dialects, Linguistic and Philological Investigations* (Amsterdam, 1986) pp. 525–83. It's an amazing, almost mathematical effort with binary pairs and the runic and alphabetic letters, but I'm afraid I agree with Sean Nowak's conclusion that in the end the argument does not quite convince or satisfy. Words are a necessary component, and not just in the rune names alone.

not yielded any convincing results."[11] Under the question of place of origin, there is some agreement that the rune shapes originated in the north Italian area, perhaps between Bolzano, Venice, and the Danube, (Raetia), thus explaining the similarities of the runes to north Etruscan forms of the Greek alphabet, but there are those who just as staunchly opt for an origin in the Latin alphabet perhaps with Celtic and ogham mediation. A west Greek proposal has been made by Alan Griffiths that may help resolve the question of the shape of the runes in the era before the creation of the fuþark.[12]

On the question of use, a communicative approach has emerged, arguing that the runes[13] were intended to be a means of communication—with the dead, with the gods, with the living. This proposal may help resolve the secular-sacred dilemma. If communication with the dead or the gods is accepted, then indeed the runes have to have magic and religious power to act and to summon, or to restrain or bind, as the bracteates and gravestones demonstrate. If communication with the living is an aim, then the runes found in Bergen and elsewhere identifying objects and their owners are good evidence for secular use as well.[14] In all of this discussion, however, the interpretation of the possible mythopoetic meaning of the rune

11. "In der Forschung hat es Versuche gegeben, die Reihenfolge des *fuþarks* aus der alphabetischen Reihenfolge herzuleiten, aber bisher ohne überzeugende Ergebnisse," *Schrift auf den Goldbrakteaten der Völkerwanderungszeit*, PhD diss. Georg-August Universtät, Göttingen, 2003. Tineke Looijenga also believes the nature of the fuþark remains unknown, "Texts and Contexts of the Oldest Runic Inscriptions," *Northern World* 4, (Leiden: Brill, 2003), p. 111.

12. Alan Griffiths, "The fuþark (and ogam): order as a key to origin." *Indogermanische Forschungen*, 104 (1999), pp. 164–211. He also suggests that concentration on social or religious circumstances might provide a more rewarding line of investigation into the order of the fuþark.

13. Christiane Zimmermann argues for the importance of the communicative context of the speech act in interpreting the runes. "Runeninschriften als Sprechakte?" in *Das fuþark* (Berlin/New York: Walter de Gruyter, 2006) pp. 434–52. She also refers to early "*Mehrsprachigkeit in den Runeninschriften im älteren Futhark,*" p. 436.

14. For an illustration of the practical, unmagical rune staves from Bergen, see Raymond I. Page, *Runes* (Berkeley: University of California Press/British Museum, 1987), p. 7.

arrangement of the fuþark seems to have been left behind with Skeat and Kluge.

First, the line of the twenty-four runes of the common elder fuþark:

ᚠ ᚢ ᚦ ᚨ ᚱ ᚲ ᚷ ᚹ ᚺ ᚾ ᛁ ᛃ ᛇ ᛈ ᛉ ᛊ ᛏ ᛒ ᛖ ᛗ ᛚ ᛜ ᛟ ᛞ

f u th a r k g w h n I j ï p R s t b e m l ng o d

From very early on this line was broken down into three aetts or families of eight runes each:

fuþarkgw:

hnijïpRs:

tbemlŋod

This division seems to have been useful primarily for cryptographic purposes.[15] If so, the needs of cryptography would also have served to fix the twenty-four runes in the order given for the sake of consistency in encoding and decoding messages and simply for making communication, in clear or in cipher, possible. Following the example of Caesar, who created a code by using every letter of the alphabet to designate a letter three places away, m, for example, actually meaning p. The fuþark was made cryptographically friendly in a parallel manner. Writing the first three runes, for example, could stand for the first three letters in the second or third aett below it. However early this useful division of the runes into three named rows might have been, it presupposed an earlier, previously existing fuþark order of the runes which it then subdivided into three groups.[16] The existence of the aetts does not really help

15. Ottar Grønvik, "Über die Bildung des älteren und jüngeren Runenalphabets" in *Osloer Beiträge zur Germanistik*, Bd. 29 (Frankfurt: Peter Lang, 2001), pp. 52–54.

16. For the opposite view, that the aetts are co-aeval with the fuþark, see Ottar Grønvik's "Über die Bildung des älteren und des jüngeren Runenalphabets" in *Osloer Beiträge zur Germanistik*, 29 (2001), pp. 50–60. On the date he gives, see p. 20, "um 170/180 n. Chr."

in attempting to explain what the previously existing fuþark meant; and if the subdivisions do not correspond to the message of the fuþark, as they do not in my opinion, the three subdivisions may actually mislead efforts at decoding the meaning of the sequence—perhaps on purpose.

Let me give an alternate subdivision of the runes in the fuþark spacing based on what I suggest is their first level of meaning. The runes for g, w, and R, have been retained in their runic form, even where the sequence is given in Roman letters, because in my reading they have added significance due to what is poetically suggested by their name or by their shape[17]:

f u þ a r
k ᚷ ᚹ h n
i j ï p ᛉ
stbe mlŋ od

Instead of families of eight for purposes of cipher, a subdivision by sense lines would, in my interpretation, fall instead into three lines of five runes and one line of nine.

The first moments of recognition for me were first, the gradual realization that several of the last letters of the sequence seemed almost to form two common Germanic words: *stbe* and *od,* "staves" and "inheritance." The second was that there appeared to be a *chi rho* in the juxtaposition of the g-rune and the w-rune, ᚷᚹ. The *chi rho* is *Christos,* Christ's Greek monogram, made famous in the Roman

17. See Bernd Neuner's perceptive reading of the Norwegian Rune Poem's use of runes for both levels, phonetic and concept, based on their shape and/or name. Especially useful is his treatment of the Norwegian h-rune as a Christ monogram in the poem. "Das norwegische Runengedicht—was sich hinter den Zeilen verbirgt," in *Runes and their Secrets: Studies in Runology,* Marie Stoklund et al., ed. (Copenhagen: Museum Tusculanum Press, University of Copenhagen, 2006), pp. 233–45, esp., 237–38.

world by Constantine's decision to use it as his battle emblem when he took the imperial throne. Then I looked at the next word to the right of it and saw *hn* and that too could be Greek, the neuter form of *eis, mia, hen,* meaning "one"—*Christos hen.* If that is so, then the *k* that precedes the ᚷᚹ can only be the abbreviation for *kai,* "and." This gives the highly unexpected ". . . and Christ are one," . . . *kai Christos hen,* an allusion that is almost a citation of John 10:30, *Ego kai ho pater hen,* "The father and I [are] one." That would make *fuþar,* the word preceding *kai,* almost have to be "father," and the meaning of the first ten runes of the fuþark becomes the words: *fuþar kai Christos hen*: "The father and Christ are one." This is an astonishing phrase to be found in the fuþark (we will discuss the possible Germanic reading of this at a later point) and it leads to considering the identity of the *fuþar.*

The u-rune in *fuþar* cannot be explained etymologically, but there may be other possibilities. Either Skeat was right about the u-rune implying *ure,* "our," for "Our Father," or it could suggest the magic word *alu* with its connotations of Woden's spellbinding power, or, and to me the most likely, it is simply the need for a nonrepeated vowel. This is a pragmatic factor based on the alphabet genre, and probably the determining one. It is the task of the creator of the fuþark, or of any alphabetic-type sequence of letters, to include all the letters or runes, but each one only once, without a repetition of any one of them—in this case without a repetition of any of the twenty-four runes. For the creator of the fuþark, however, the task was more difficult because of his need to balance the single-use requirement with the need to create his ten words without admitting excessive phonetic distortion. This calls for a runemaster skilled at balance. Thus in the case of the first vowel of *fuþar* the u-rune here might simply have been the most amenable and least distorting placement. The a-rune cannot be repeated as it is in the actual word *fathar.* The internal *u* in this spot may also have had the advantage of suggesting an appropriate note of hallowedness, whether the fourth-century runemaster was thinking of *ure* or *alu,* or both, in connection with father. We will return to the question of the identity of the father when we consider the Vadstena bracteate.

I was completely taken aback, not only by the presence of a Greek phrase, but more by what the words said. If this decipherment is accurate, what is this phrase from John's Gospel doing in Woden's runes? We may have stumbled upon another surprising example of Late Antiquity's syncretism.

Years before I had been fascinated by two words that I thought could be identified near the end of the rune sequence. Examining the last two runes of the fuþark we see a common and quickly recognizable Germanic word, ᛟᛞ, "od," or "hereditary property." In English, the word takes the form "ed" as in the familiar name Ed-ward, "homestead guardian." "Od" or its variants would be intelligible, as are the other common Germanic words of the fuþark, across the spectrum of the Germanic world of the North because the words are basic vocabulary.

Examination of the runes just prior to the word "od" should reveal just what it is that constitutes the hereditary property, that is: ᛊᛏᛒᛖ, or, supplying the missing "a" vowel, "staves," wooden sticks, or in modern German, *Stäbe.* The three staves, or runes, that follow **s t b e,** are ᛗᛚᛜ, or **m l ŋ**, which are a form of the Germanic root *mahlian* (Old Saxon) "to speak" or "to talk"; the word in Old Norse being *mæla* with the adjective *málig,* "talking" or "talkative." The ng-rune here is used for its full "ng" value with an emphasis on the "g" to qualify the nature of the staves as *málig* or "talking."[18]

18. The g-rune and the k-rune have already occurred in the sequence, hence neither can be used here for the final g of *málig.*

The "hereditary property," then, is "sticks that speak" or "talking staves," ᛊᛏᛒᛖ ᛗᛚᛜ ᛟᛞ. This is a remarkably accurate description of the runes especially in the light of their being inscribed on wooden sticks or staves and one of their several uses being to "tell" whose property a thing is, as in the wooden staves uncovered at Bergen. Far more, however, the runes speak by telling and foretelling the future when they are cast into a white cloth three times, then collected and read (cf. *lesen*) by a rune reader who first prays to the gods and looks up to the heavens as he gathers them up in a procedure described so famously in the first century, AD 98, by Tacitus in his *Germania (10)*:

> Auspicia sortesque ut qui maxime observant. sortium consuetudo simplex, virgam frugiferae arbori decissam in surculos amputant eosque notis quibusdam discretos super candidam vestam temere ac fortuito spargunt, mox . . . precatus deos caelumque suspiciens, ter singulos tollit, sublatos secundum impressam ante notam interpretatur.

In a ritual gesture parallel to Woden's grasping the runes, "they cut off (*decissam*[19] [modifies *virgam*]) a shoot or branch (*virgam*) of a living tree, then they lop off (*amputant*)[20] young twigs (*surculos*) from it and put letters [or signs] (*notae*) on them." There has

19. From *de-cido, decidere* "to cut off, cut from, cut down, prune." A *virga decissa* is then a cut-off branch or stick. [Harper's Latin Dictionary]

20. From *am-puto, amputare,* "to cut around, cut off, trim; to amputate." Both *decissam* and *amputant* are in accord with the notion of "cut, or cut off" implied in the Old Norse *skíđi.* Ursula Dronke in her commentary on *skáro á skđi* is mistaken when she maintains that Tacitus's use of *decidere* and *amputare* implies "plucking" twigs from a living tree rather than cutting them from it." The common use of both verbs in Latin is "to cut off" [Harper's], exactly as is implied in the Old Norse *skíði*. Cf. Her commentary on the *Voluspa* in *The Poetic Edda,* vol. II, *Mythological Poems* (Oxford: Clarendon, 1997), p. 128.

been so much argument over the meaning of *notae,* whether they are really runes, proto-runes, or symbols, that the tree and the ritual of cutting and marking the sticks or staves has been overlooked. These little twigs, *surculi,* sticks or staves, are expected, following the pattern of the myth of Woden, to be able to "speak" to the interpreter in the ritual who in turn has received the gift from Woden of being able to understand their content and thereby foretell the future.

In the Elder Edda there is a passage in the *Völuspá* (19, 20) which explains how the rune staves could have such knowledge carved on them: they were carved on the sticks by the Norns who arise from the well of Urd and who water the tree Yggdrasil.

> I know that there stands an ash-tree
> Called Yggdrasil,
> A high tree, soaked with shining loam;
> From there come the dews
> That fall in the valley.
> Ever green, it stands over
> The well of Fate.
> . . . .
> From there come the maidens,
> Knowing a great deal,
> Three of them, out of the lake,
> Which stands under the tree.
> They call one Urd ["what happened"]
> The second Verdandi ["what is happening"]
> —they carved on a stave—
> The third Skuld ["what shall happen"].
> They established laws,
> They chose lives

For the children of people,
Fates of men.

(Translation modified from John Lindow,
Norse Mythology, p. 244.)

The simple line "they carved on a cut-off stick/stave," *scáro á sciđi,* is inserted between the second and third Norn. The insertion of "carved on a cut-off stick" is not only in remarkable correspondence with the ritual magic described in the text of Tacitus, but also by the position of this insertion among the Norns, between the Norn of the present and the Norn of the future. The line clearly suggests in poetic form that the origin of the runes' power in the present to foretell the happenings of the future lies with the time knowledge of the three Norns. The small carved sticks/staves, cut-off twigs of Yggdrasil, the tree of life under which the Norns have their place and function, are marked with runic signs (Tacitus' *notae*) by the three forces that control "laws and lives" and the destinies of men: the Norns, the women who emerge from Urd, the well of time past, who water the trunk of the tree, coating the bark with the white loam of aging, giving life and time to its branches and twigs, and carving readable runes on the twigs they have removed from it.

Returning now to the middle section of the fuþark, between the runes that (on one level) spell out "The father and Christ are one" and "talking staves, hereditary property," comes the common verb of "giving," *geban* in Old Saxon, with, I believe, a preceding adverb and a following indirect object:

ᛁᛃᛇᛈᛉ, i j ï p R. The three central runes, ᛃᛇᛈ / j ï p, are recognizable as a basic form of the verb to give. "Gift" in Old Norse is *gib-t,*pronounced (jip-t), and very close to the j-i-p runes above, as is the past tense of the verb to present a gift: *gipta.* In all these cases the g of "give" or *giefan* (Old English) was pronounced as a j (y).

The j-rune is thus appropriate for a phonetic spelling of a word beginning with a soft g, like *giefan*.[21] The yew-rune, ᛇ, always somewhat troublesome to nail down, stands for a vowel in the 'e' to the 'ä' to 'æ' range thus giving a *jæp jep* or *jip* phonetic reading to the central three runes. The final p-rune is appropriate in the North, and I believe final p-rune would have been adequately intelligible outside Scandinavia in regions that would have used an f.

The rune that precedes the j, i, p runes is the i-rune. It is probably most simply read as standing for the common Germanic *io*, which can mean many things, all related to duration of time, such as "once (in the past)," "ever," or "always" and is probably best understood here as "long ago."[22]

The rune that follows ᛃᛇᛈ is the slippery ᛉ, or R-rune. Over the course of time it seems to have had phonetic values ranging from an original "z" sound through a voiceless "r" to an "m" sound. Its runic name *algiz is unclear, though it could mean "elk," and that would explain its upper "branches" as elk's antlers. The R-rune in the North, however, seems to have been taken as representing a person (with two arms extended [and in some versions this rune also has two extended legs]). The Scandinavian name for this rune is *maðr*, meaning "human being." This usage is found in the Norwegian Rune Poem. The R-rune as a "z" or a voiceless "r" seems unneeded here in a phonetic capacity, and so I think even if used for an "a" ending, it is properly read here as a *Begriffsrune* or ideogram, a rune that can stand not only for its sound but also for what its name or shape suggests, here: a human being.

21. My purpose here is not to establish fourth-century pronunciation, but simply to indicate through the later Old Saxon and Old English and Old Norse, that the use of the j-rune in the fourth-century fuþark seems phonetically appropriate for the soft g sound. In any case the g-rune has already been used in the sequence and is therefore ineligible here.

22. Duden, *Herkunftswörterbuch*, under "je" refers to this word as a common-Germanic adverb of time, and gives as variants Old English *ā*, Old Icelandic *æ*, Old High German *io*, and Gothic *aiw*. It is related to the modern German *ewig*. In Old Saxon and Old Norse it is *io*.

We now have the central part of the fuþark: ᛁᛃ ᛇᛈ ᛉ, ". . . long ago gave mankind . . ." and therefore we can now give a full reading, non-Germanic part in italics, of the rune sequence:

ᚠᚢᚦᚨᚱ ᚲ ᚷᚹ ᚺᚾ ᛁ ᛃᛇᛈ ᛉ ᛊᛏᛒᛖ ᛗᛚᛜ ᛟᛞ.
fuþar *kai Christos hen* io jïp maðr stabe maliŋ od

"Father *and Christ [are] one*, long ago gave mankind speaking staves, hereditary property."

This first possible solution to the riddle of the fuþark reveals a closeness of its message to the myth itself in which the origin of the runes is revealed as a gift of Woden/Odin seized from the tree Yggdrasil, as found illustrated in the c-class fuþark bracteates, as told in the Elder Edda, and as elaborated by Snorri Sturluson centuries later, in a long continuity.[23] This solution also brings to light the remarkable observation by the fuþark master that Christ is the coauthor with "father." And why is that part left in biblical Greek? The reader will have noticed that if the Greek is left out, the line reads, "**Father . . . long ago gave talking staves to man as hereditary property.**" There can be no doubt that Woden/Odin is the father being referred to, the All-father who in the Havamal (138, 139) hanged himself from the cosmic tree of life, Yggdrasil, hanging for nine nights until he reached out and seized the runes and then, screaming, fell back:

I know that I hung on a windy tree
nine long nights,

23. One might add that a pedagogical situation, requiring memorization of the twenty-four runes, would be a very appropriate context for using an encoded version of the myth of Odin's divine gift of the runes. For more on the relationship between myth, memory, and context, see Carolyne Larrington, "Myth and the Psychology of Memory," in *Old Norse Religion in Long-term Perspectives, Origins, Changes, and Interactions*. Anders Andrén et al., eds. (Lund: Nordic Academic Press, 2006), pp. 272–75.

wounded with a spear, dedicated to Odin,
myself to myself,
on that tree of which no man knows
from where its roots run.
No bread did they give me nor drink from a horn,
downwards I peered;
I took up the runes, screaming I took them,
then I fell back from there."

(Translation from Carolyne Larrington,
The Poetic Edda, p. 34.)

Christ in his own story must have been seen by the runemaster who created the fuþark as a parallel to the hanged god, Woden. Christ also hung from the tree and gave his blood as a communion from the tree of the cross. Woden gave the powerful runes, Christ gave powerful words, and is himself, in John's Gospel the Logos, the divine word of creation. If we take the ninth-century *Heliand* as indicative of a Germanic appreciation of the story of Christ and words, the poet is amazed primarily at the power of the "light words" used by Christ in speaking. The *Heliand*'s first song expresses amazement that in the beginning Christ made the whole world with one powerful word ("*fiat*" in the Vulgate). He used powerful words to calm the storm and "to give great magic power" to the bread and wine at the last supper. In other words, the fuþark poet must have seen the magic power of Woden and his divine rune-letters as quite parallel to that of Jesus and his divine words. Indeed it seems from the first words of the fuþark that he was aware of John's gospel. He would have been impressed by its beginning: "In the beginning was the word and the word was with God, and the word was God."

Letters and words are not hostile to each other, they are complementary, and in this sense, both Woden and Christ hung from the cosmic tree of life, both bled, stabbed with the spear, and from the tree were benefactors of mankind in the realm of communication and communion. One gave men the powerful magic of letters, the other the powerful magic of words and the Word. It is from this kind of spiritual conflation, I believe, that the religious runemaster of the first fuþark, could have said that Woden and Christ are one. The poet who created the fuþark then left a poetic monument to his two sources. Unlike all alphabets before him which embodied one language, his fuþark embodied two. Unlike all alphabets before him which consisted of letters only, his consisted of rune-letters that had become words, runes able to speak words.

It is not surprising that the runes, which are a Germanic use of Mediterranean letters, should also come accompanied by Germanic use of Mediterranean content, the story of Christ. One can only speculate, as I have above, as to why the fuþark author felt it appropriate to keep the Christ statement in its original language. Perhaps because of magic reasons, or perhaps, as I also suggested before, to act as a barrier to someone uninitiated attempting to read the fuþark beyond the word *fuþar*—perhaps also because not everyone shared his synthetic view of the All-father and Christ being one in contributing to communication through signs. There is a built-in ambiguity as to the identity of the father in the first five runes. Is this father the God the Father of Jesus Christ, as the possible allusion to John's Gospel (10:30) would seem to indicate, or is it the Germanic All-father Woden, giver of the runes, as the rest of the rune sequence indicates; or would the fuþark creator like to preserve the ambiguity of his mythic synthesis, but keep the ambiguity safe from the prying eyes of the overly zealous and well-armed Christian or Germanic pagan? In any case, the Greek Christian part of the fuþark, though intelligible to the initiate in the East, very soon must have been undecipherable to pagan

Nordic rune readers. Its five runes must have been consigned to the mysterious and unintelligible, and most likely, a Germanic reading given to them, an alternate level of meaning that I believe the author had also built into the five runes.[24] Finally, what no one would doubt is the fuþark master's acceptance of the divine origin of runic letters-and-words as being one. The runes are *raginokundo*, they come from the gods. The *Fuþar* of words and letters is both *alu* and *hagios*.

Figure 6.1. Gotland's Kylver stone, dated to approximately 400 AD, showing the underside of the lid stone on which the runes of the elder fuþark run from left to right. At the end of the line is a stylized drawing of a pine tree which I interpret as Yggdrasil, and further to the right, just outside the photo, the letters SUEUS, which have been read as possibly being a palindrome for eus, "horse." Each of the three items in the inscription seem related to the mythology of the evergreen tree Yggdrasil as Woden's horse, "riding" on which he seized the runes. (The first three runes are beyond the photo's left edge.) From the Statens Historiska Museet, Stockholm, Sweden. Werner Forman/Art Resource, NY.

24. We will return at the end of this chapter to consider what this might have been.

The syncretism in the fuþark would thus indicate a double religious power source for the magic of the runes, both Woden and Christ. It is for this reason, perhaps, that for the runes to reach their full ritual effectiveness, they needed to be cut from a living tree, then carved, and then painted with blood, or blood and water, or a red color. More than Woden, whose runes are powerful even before he seizes them while hanging on the tree, Christ's words come to take effect in the shedding of his blood. Putting blood, or its near equivalent, on the runes during runic magical ritual, may actually not be so much imitative of Woden, as much as an attempt to give the runes the life/death power of Christ. This part of runic ritual may be indebted as much to the story of Christ as to that of Woden, but that was also soon forgotten if it was ever realized. The runes themselves in their fourth-century fuþark speak and tell the same story as Snorri and the Elder Edda, confirming that the runes come from the All-father, from Woden and ultimately the tree.

Who is the religious runemaster who composed the fuþark? Of course he is lost in the very distant past and we will never know his identity. What we can speculate about beyond his ecumenical and synthetic poetic pattern, one common enough to Late Antiquity, is: what made him want to do this? I believe he was answering a question that might have come up for him if he was a Germanic runemaster from the North who found himself in positive contact with Eastern Christianity and possible conversion, wondering if it was really appropriate for him to continue using Woden's magic letters, especially if, as he shows, Greek letters were also a possibility for him. This is all the more a pressing question, if, as Klaus Düwel emphatically maintains,[25] the very act of rune-writing was itself

25. On the subject of colored runes he writes, "Auch hier haben wir also wieder ein Beispiel dafür, daß der Akt des Schreibens selbst—des Runenschreibens!—als magische Handlung empfunden wurde: Schriftzauber." "Runeninschrift auf einem 'Schemel' aus einem

was a religious action stemming from a Woden-given ability. As a Germanic Christian, perhaps an Orthodox or Arian Goth, should he not be using a "Christian alphabet?" This is the question that Wulfila must have been wary of when he declined to use more than a few of Woden's runes in his fourth-century translation of the bible into Gothic. The fuþark master's poetic answer to this question is the fuþark. Woden, the father, and Christ, are one. There is one father who gave human beings the magic ability to hear both the Germanic runes speak, as well as Greco-Roman letters; one and the same paternal source shared with mankind the divine ability to read writing as a family inheritance.

Now let us examine this reading in light of the contexts supplied by two of the earliest fuþark inscriptions, the Swedish Kylver stone (see Figure 6.1) and the Danish Vadstena bracteate (Figure 6.2a). There are, of course, earlier objects that use runes, such as the comb from the Vimose bog on Funen in Denmark with the inscription **harja,** "warrior,"[26] or some say "hair comb," or possibly the owner's name, and it has been dated to approximately AD 160. The first full fuþark listing all twenty-four runes is not found until approximately AD 400 and then again in AD 450–500. This may be due simply to the perishability of wood producing an absence during the intervening period, and it could also mean that the fuþark's arrangement of the runes was a later development. Originally when teaching or learning the runes, other, perhaps more directly alphabetical sequences, might have served quite well until a rune listing

Bootgrab bei Wremen," In *Nytt om runer* 9, pp. 14–16. Cited by Ute Schwab, "Runen der Merowingerzeit als Quelle für das Weiterleben der spätantiken christlichen und nichtchristlichen Schriftmagie," *Runeninschriften als Quellen interdsiziplinärer Forschung; Abhandlungen des Vierten Internationalen Symposiums über Runen und Runeninschriften* (Berlin: Walter de Gruyter, 1998), pp. 376–433.

26. I am indebted to Prof. James Cathey of the University of Massachusetts, Amherst, for this reading. He traces the word *harja* to the I-E word *koryos, "warrior."

was created using the Germanic story of their origin as its basis.[27] That the story of the runes' origin is the basis of the fuþark sequence is, of course, my thesis.

The Kylver stone was found covering a grave on the island of Gotland, Sweden. Inscribed on it is the full fuþark and an added pine or spruce tree incised as if it were an additional rune in the row. There is also a curious palindromic riddle ᛊᚢᛖᚢᛊ, **sueus**, carved on the stone that Marstrander has interpreted as meaning *eus*, "horse." It would seem that the purpose of such a stone has something to do with the dead man, but it seems this is not the case. There is nothing in the inscription to indicate an attempt to bind the dead man to the grave, and the magic word **alu** that one might expect to find in such a case is absent. There are also many irregularities in the inscription. Three runes are written backwards, a, s, and b, compared to the rest of the runes in the sequence. The sequence of several of the runes is off, including the final **od** which is written **do**. This word is so obvious that I think the transposition must have been done deliberately. Though some scholars believe the mistakes are just the result of an amateur repeating the mistakes disparaged in the Egil's Saga, I think these are more than the mistakes of an inept *Stümper*, as one scholar put it. The inscribed fuþark may indeed be the work of a learner, but I think it is the work of a ritually very careful beginner. One of the first clues to this is that the first rune itself, the **f** of **fuþar,** is misdone. It seems even a clumsy learner should get the first letter right, and yet the vertical staff is standing there in position but with the two oblique branches missing. And then the w-rune in the ᚷᚹ combination is missing its loop (though some editors insert it), but the vertical

27. For further discussion, see Bengt Odenstedt, *On the Origin and Early History of the Runic Script, Typology and Graphic Variation in the older* Fuþark (Uppsala/Stockholm: Almquist & Wiksell International, 1990), esp. pp. 168–73.

staff is there.[28] By leaving the vertical staff in position, the carver wants you to know this "forgetfulness" is on purpose. It is not that he forgot the letter, he is rather deliberately disabling it. It seems he might have been afraid that in writing out the fuþark he might be calling up, unintentionally, the owner and donor of its powerful letter magic, Woden (and Christ). Thus he disables the powerful f-rune that refers to Woden and the *rho* of the w-rune referring to Christ. Similar things were done in Egyptian magic with "dangerous" images on the wall inside the tomb being partially defaced, and thereby disabled, to protect the soul of the dead from harm. Then the Kylver stone carver disables the order of the runes as an additional precaution. He is telling the gods that he is only practicing. He is not the sorcerer's apprentice and does not wish to call up the All-father, or Christ.

Most important is that the attempt to disable shows that the carver is aware of the presence of magic power in the staves of the fuþark, and that the one who gave them is Woden. In a nice poetic gesture he carves the evergreen tree that is always over Mimir's well "whose roots no one knows," at the end of the rune row. He makes the tree, Yggdrasil, from which Woden hung and seized the runes, be present at the right-hand end of the very rune row in which the words "gave the speaking staves" appear—Yggdrasil and the fuþark, side by side. Not far away, but rather later in time, the same stylized form of the evergreen tree can be found in the Skog tapestry at the church in Sweden, where it serves as of old to identify the figure of Odin/Woden. Woden was hanging from the tree when he sacrificed himself and reached out to seize the runes. Though the myth doesn't

28. Sigurd Agrell said that the ᚹ, the w-rune, is very hard to see. He said others had seen traces of the loop, and he himself tried to feel for it. If there, it is very faintly carved. He too felt that there is an attempt to disable the rune-row. "Die spätantike Alphabetmystik und die Runenreihe," in (same title) no. 6 (1931–1932), pp. 155–210.

Figures 6.2a and 6.2b. The Vadstena brakteate from Sweden and the Lindkær from Denmark are dated at approximately 500 AD. Both are c-type bracteates depicting Woden riding his horse with one or both of his ravens, Hugin and Munin (mind and memory), whispering in his ear. The runes of the fuþark encircle Woden as he rides, suggesting their connection to the god. In the Vadstena bracteate, one of the ravens is standing on a "branch," which is a part of the horse on which Woden is mounted: the tree Yggdrasil. The Lindkær medal goes further by having the rune sequence constitute the actual bodies of the birds, Hugin and Munin. The fuþark reads counter-clockwise from upper left to right on both bracteates, somewhat irregularly on the Lindkaer. Significantly associating the function of the runes with mind and memory, on the Lidkær medal the rune sequence begins and ends with the birds' heads. Drawings by Laurence Selim.

normally specify where these staves were seized from, both the account of Tacitus and the Kylver carving serve to suggest an answer. Woden, the hanging god, was seizing magic staves, talking twigs with runes carved on them by the three Norns, from the Tree of Life itself, Yggdrasil. Whoever carved the palindromic horse riddle, **sueus**, ("horse" is *eus* in two directions)[29] over the fuþark tree on the Kylver stone (if it was not the carver himself) must have been aware as well of the connection of the fuþark's "talking staves" to Yggdrasil, since to the tree he added the horse, Woden's horse, thereby giving the observer another clue to what he is seeing: Ygg-drasil, the "Awesome One's horse." The fuþark rune sequence simply echoes and confirms the myth of Woden and Yggdrasil. That is, that when he rode the tree of life in death, the awesome One seized the talking twigs from it and, dying, gave them to men as a their inheritance from him.

The connection between the message of the fuþark and the image of Woden is seen even more cleverly in several of the bracteates that have been found in Denmark, most famously in the impressive work of art called the Vadstena bracteate. This medal, dated to about AD 500, was found at Vadsten in Denmark. Its fuþark is complete with only a repetition of the b-rune for the p-rune in the sequence. Scholars generally do not examine the image as much as the runes, but I think there is a distinct relationship between the two. As opposed to the Kylver stone runes, the sequence is normal; no runes have been reversed in direction or sequence, so the wearer wanted to invoke the presence and the power of the god and his runes. The runes form a circular border for the central image, which depicts the head of a man—the eye depicted on the observer's side appears to be blind—riding his horse at high speed.[30] It has to be Woden/Odin.

29. I am indebted to Marstrander for this interpretation of **sueus**.
30. The opinion has been expressed that the c-type bracteates' image of a man's head floating over a horse, or ox, may have been influenced by the Roman cultic image of Mithras

The tongue of the horse is sticking out and curled down as if the horse were being ridden hard. The hair too of the man, tied in a curious knot, is sticking out behind as if moving through the air at high speed. There is a bird clutching a twig in its foot as it speaks into Woden's ear. The artist has nicely suggested that the bird is speaking into Woden's ear by having part of its beak disappear behind Woden's hair. The bird, of course has to represent Hugin and Munin,

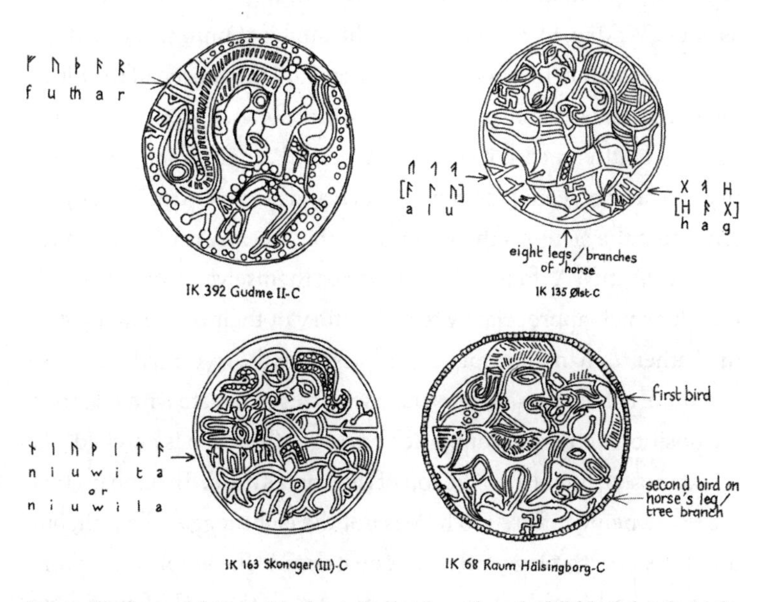

Figures 6.3a, b, c, and d. Four c-type bracteates that do not have the full fuþark, but depict the rotating motion of Woden riding the cosmic tree, the Awesome One's horse, in the night sky, by showing swastikas and three-pointed stars. The raven hovers near his face. IK 135 Ølst-c has the inscription a l u, "alu," below left in Germanic and h a g, "hag," below right, possibly short for "hagios" in Greek. Both words would then mean "holy," in Germanic and in Greek. The 163 Skonager (III)-c bracteate has an inscription below the horse's head under the raven which reveals what the bird whispers in Woden's ear: n i u w i t[l] a, "niu wita" or "niu wila," "new knowledge, news"; or "new time, new tidings." The 68 Raum Hälsingborg-c bracteate has two ravens present, showing in their way that the "horse" is Yggdrasil: the first bird is perched on the familiar branch above the horse's head, the second is on a branch that is one of the horse's "forelegs." The upper left bracteate, 392 Gudme II-c, has a quotation of the first five runes of the fuþark, fuþar, placed next to the large head, indicating, I believe, the identity of the horse's rider as the all-father, Woden. Drawings by Laurence Selim.

mind and memory, the two ravens who fly about in the world and come back in the evening to tell the chief god what is happening.

Just how do mind and memory inform the god? The raven speaks into his ear and says (now we turn to the writing in runes on the edge of the bracteate), "tuwa, tuwa." To many, this must be a secret magic formula. For me this is not so much a secret magic word repeated, but rather an imitation of how ravens and crows speak. We may prefer, "caw, caw" in imitating corvids, but I think "tuWA, tuWA" is just as good. Woden, like Siegfried after he put his thumb with the dragon's blood on it in his mouth, can understand the speech of the birds. However the bird is also clutching a stick, a branch, in its feet which it brings to utterance as it speaks to Woden. Woden's mind and memory, the ravens, seeing the runes, clutch and read aloud, magically interpreting the signs on the sticks from the Tree. Next of course after the "tuWA, tuWA" follow the very runes themselves arranged in the fuþark, which appropriately tells the story of their origin as a gift of the Father to mankind: speaking staves from the tree Yggdrasil.

The artist has done a nice touch with this bracteate with regard to the position of the stick or branch on which the raven is perched—it is juxtaposed, literally, to the top of the horse's head. That means that the horse being referred to here is not the eight-legged Sleipnir, but the "horse," with twigs and ravens on its head. The whole medallion, its image and its fuþark, is not only a call to the god of awareness to be aware of, and come quickly to the aid of, the wearer, perhaps helping with interpreting runes, it is also a kenning. It is a visual riddle to be solved, much in the vein of an Anglo-Saxon riddle: "What

stabbing the bull. It seems, however, that there are too many differences, such as the high-speed racing of the horse and the lack of a sacrificial stabbing, for this to be significant in the interpretation of the medal. Cf. Anders Kaliff and Olof Sundquist, "Odin and Mithras, Religious acculturation during the Roman Iron Age and the Migration Period," in *Old Norse Religion in Long-term Perspectives, Origins, Changes, and Interactions*, pp. 212–17.

do I portray, with magic talking sticks all in a row, speaking ravens who tell tales to the most high, and a god who rides me as his horse. And, though I join all to all, I am invisible, and, as on this bracteate, am not to be seen by men. Who am I?" (Yggdrasil).

What Tacitus did not add about the ritual was that the fruitful tree from which the twigs were taken and inscribed with early runes and symbols had to be a living tree, evergreen, since it represented the fact that the branches were taken from the cosmic tree of life, Yggdrasil—which immediately calls up the image of Woden on the bracteate. He is a depiction of the magic of reading and of the craft of the rune carver and reader. The transformation from the carved rune or symbol on the stick to vocalization and comprehension is represented by the action of the symbolic figure of the bird. The bird sees and feels the rune-twig and expresses it (tuWA, tu WA) and Woden comprehends the meaning of the signs and puts them into words. The fuþark is the listing of the signs, and the expression of the belief, that the ability of human beings to interpret signs, to read, is a divine gift. Surely these medallions would have been something that a runemaster, or anyone who could read, would proudly wear.

There have been recent finds at Roskilde in Denmark that also confirm this interpretation of the relation of the fuþark sequence to the myth of Woden.[31] The Lindkaer and Overhornbeck bracteates both put the runes of the fuþark on the edge of the bracteate, but enclose them inside of a long strip which becomes a two-headed bird, one head at the beginning and one and the end of the rune-row (Figure 6.2b). In both bracteates the head of Woden, riding his horse,

31. They are nicely illustrated in Karl Hauck and Wilhelm Heizmann's "Der Neufund des Runen-Brakteaten IK 585 Sankt Ibs Vej-C Roskilde," in *Runica Germanica Mediaevalia* Band 37 (Berlin/New York: Walter de Gruyter, 2003), pp. 244–64.

See also Elmar Seebold's "Das *fuþark* auf den Brakteaten-Inschriften," in *Das fuþark* (Berlin/New York: Walter de Gruyter, 2006), pp. 157–67. His concern is for older rune forms on the bracteates possibly also illustrating older variants of the common fuþark.

is directly below the beaks of the ravens. The different sequences of the runes in these fuþarks are evidence, Seebold maintains, that there were different forms, possibly, from the standard fuþark sequence. I could not agree more, though I think in this case, the runes are more symbolic of the random speech capabilities of Hugin and Munin and the great ability of Woden to comprehend what they tell him in mysterious, runic language. (See Figures 6.3a–d.) A nice example is the IK 163 Skonager (III)-c bracteate in which the raven is shown speaking face to face with Woden while under the horse's head is the runic inscription ᚾᛁᚢ ᚹᛁᛏᚨ, "*niu wita*." The bird speaks the fuþark-runes to the god, bringing him "new knowledge," or simply "news," of what is going on in the world.[32]

Perhaps even more exciting for me, are the signs of the awareness on the part of the artists of these bracteates that Woden's horse is really the tree from which the fuþark comes.[33] If one examines the IK 135 Ølst-c bracteate, it is ingenious how the artist has the observer first see the Awesome One's horse as Sleipnir with his eight legs, but then if you examine the highly modernist handling of the four legs and you see that each one of them is really a thin branch of a tree, which divides into two twigs at the end. Also in the image are stars and two swastikas, ensuring that the ride that the god takes is a cosmic one circling around, as the swastikas indicate, the north star of the heavens. The bird is present, foot on a branch, speaking

32. The branch of the t-rune in *wita* is reversed, or is possibly an "l." If the word is then *wila*, the bird is bringing word of "new time" or "new tidings," or "news."

33. Hauck and Heizmann (see previous) have an alternate interpretation. They see the bracteates as (medical-healing) amulets, and thus identify the horse on the disk as Balder's foal being healed by Woden, rather than Yggdrasil being ridden by the god, despite the clear presence of the birds and branches. They also see the form "fuþar"on brakteate IK 392 Gudme II-c as an abbreviation for fuþark, but miss its function as an identification of the Woden figure. I see the writing of "fuþar" directly behind the head of the Woden as evidence that the designer of the image realized that the first five runes of the fuþark refer to Woden, and as "father."

to Woden. The "horse" is flying on its branches, while runes at the bottom—nicely associated with the branches of the horse's legs—correctly say *alu* and *hag*. *Alu* is familiar as "holy," *hag* is not. I think I would know with whom to associate this bracteate, however, if the *hag* was short for the Greek word "holy," *hagios*, here standing in parallel to *alu*.

The bracteate IK 68 Hälsingborg has two birds. One is above the horse's head, feet wrapped around a curved branch of the horse's head as he speaks with Woden, and the second bird is perched on a branch below, a leg, indicating that the racing front "leg" of the horse really is the branch of the tree. The artists all seem quite aware that in drawing Woden's mount, they are depicting Yggdrasil and its rune staves, the perfect environment for the fuþark on the edge of the bracteate.

A last word on place and time. If this decipherment of the fuþark sequence is correct, then its Greek and Germanic, Christian and pagan harmony, point to a Swedish runemaster in contact with the Greek-speaking Eastern Roman Empire and possibly a syncretistic Germanic-Christian himself. Though the runes themselves may have originated in the north italian area, by the second century they were in Denmark, see **harja** above, AD 160. However, the first arrangement we have of the runes in the fuþark sequence comes from Gotland [Goth-land], Sweden, two hundred and fifty years later. Before the fuþark was devised there may well have been other mnemonic devices used to transmit the runes as a whole, possibly even alphabetic ones based on the sources, but there is no trace of a fuþark sequence until the Kylver stone inscription of AD 400, and it shows up on the Swedish island of Gotland.[34] The Fuþark may thus be a fourth-century invention, as we have proposed, coming out of

34. A possible place to look for earlier, more alphabetic, rune sequences would be on bracteates with images of Woden and with twenty-four non-repeating runes.

the intersection of Gothic-Scandinavian contact with the Eastern Roman Empire. We propose Swedish contacts rather than Danish or Norwegian because of the possible presence of a Gothic ritual phrase in the fuþark and also because the Swedes tended to trade toward Constantinople and the Greek East rather than toward the Latin West. The runemaster might have been a Goth from the trading island of Gotland who had gone east with his goods, bringing his runes, however arranged, and his mythology, with him.[35]

As to the time, I think it might be appropriate to think of the time of Constantine and the decree of universal (not just Christian) toleration. The Edict of Milan was an attempt by both Roman emperors, Latin and Greek, in AD 313 to establish the favor of heaven for both parts of the empire. Christians who had been dispossessed or suffered other losses were to have them be restored by the magistrates, but more important, all the gods above, and not just the God of the Christians or those of the pagans, were to be recognized without prejudice so as to bring their universal good will upon the whole empire:

> When I, Constantine Augustus, and well as I, Licinius Augustus, fortunately met near Mediolanum (Milan), and were considering everything that pertained to the public welfare and security, we thought, among other things that would be for the good of many, that those regulations pertaining to the reverence of the Divinity (*quibus divinitatis reverentia continebatur*) ought certainly to be made first, so that we might grant to the Christians and to all (et Christianis et omnibus) full authority to observe that religious

35. This theory was proposed by Isaac Taylor in the nineteenth century, who consistently called the elder fuþark the Gothic fuþark, and saw the runes as a creation of the Goths in their interaction with the Byzantine Roman Empire. See his *Greeks and Goths: A Study on the Runes* (Breinigsville, PA: Nabu Press, 2011 [original Oxford: 1879]). His treatment of the order of the runes, however, as an adapted alphabetic sequence is much too spare to be persuasive.

> reverence which each preferred toward any Divinity whatsoever enthroned in the heavens (quicquid divinitatis in sede caelesti) that the Divinity may be propitious and pleased with us and with all who are under our rule. [The emperors then add a practical note familiar in our time on the reason for respecting all religions equally:] We have also conceded to other religions the right of open and free practice of their worship for the sake of peace in our times (pro quietate temporis nostri).[36] [transl. modified]

It is in this tolerant spirit perhaps, in the early to midfourth century, that the Germanic runes that had existed since the second century were composed into the generous and tolerant fuþark sequence: "**Father and Christ were one long ago in giving mankind speaking staves as hereditary property**:"

ᚠᚢᚦᚨᚱ · ᚲ · ᚷᚹ · ᚺᚾ · ᛁ · ᛃᛇᛈ · ᛉ · ᛊᛏᛒᛖ · ᛗᛚᛜ · ᛟᛞ.

This may be the point to give a final consideration to the second line of five runes, runes six to ten. It seems that to serve as a good mnemonic aid they, in the style of the Norse Rune Poem, should also make sense in Germanic as well as in Greek. The line seems at first to resist such a reading; however the sequence of consonants, k, g, w, h, n, could perhaps have been read, inserting the vowels as follows, "*auk gaweihnai*" to make sense in Gothic, and rather surprisingly familiar sense at that. The conjunction "*auk*" can be rendered by "for," or "and." "*Weihnan*" is the verb[37] used in Wulfila's

36. Both Latin and English can be found on the web: English—http://gbgm-umc.org/UMW/Bible/milan.stm, Latin—http://web.upmf-grenoble.fr//Haiti/Cours/Ak/Constitutiones/ed_tolerat1.htm.

37. For the following discussion I am dependent on Wilhelm Braune's treatment of the function of "-nan" verbs, which are intransitive, inchoative verbs and are used in Gothic to translate the Greek middle voice. The adjective *weihs* means holy, but the verb *weihnan*

Gothic bible translation (c. 350 AD) for the first petition of the Lord's prayer, "*weihnai namo thein,*" "hallowed be thy name." This verb does not seem to attest the perfective prefix "*ga-,*" although the prefix is present in parallel "*-nan*" verbs, such as "*gahailnan,*" "to become sound or healthy." It may be that the creator of the sequence wanted a Germanic series of runes in the second line that would also be compatible with a Greek reading of them. If so, he needed a runic ᚷ to be the "Chi" for the Chi-Rho figure, ᚷ ᚹ, so that the five runes could also make sense in the Greek reading of the line—and thus he might have needed the "*ga*" prefix. I have appended the third-person singular optative verb ending "*ai*" from Wulfila. The conclusion is that the second line of five runes could possibly have been read *auk gaweihnai,* a parenthetic expression perhaps echoing the first petition of Wulfila's Paternoster, and would mean: "may he be held holy," or "and hallowed be he." The entire fuþark sequence could then also be read by the Germanic speaking learner who had little or no Greek, as directly celebrating Germanic mythology's tale of Yggdrasil and the All-father's gift of the runes but also containing an unexpected and perhaps unperceived overtone of a Christian prayer:[38]

> "Father, and hallowed be he, long ago gave mankind talking staves, hereditary property."

It would appear that Skeat's suggestion of 1890, that there was some relationship between the Lord's Prayer and the sequence of

is not to consecrate something, but rather to become holy. See his *Gotische Grammatik, mit Lesestücken und Wörterverzeichnis, 16. Auflage, neu bearbeitet von Ernst Ebbinghaus* (Tübingen: Niemeyer, 1961), pp. 114–16.

38. This is found later in the *Heliand's* charming introduction to the Lord's Prayer: "*girihti us that giruni,*" "Teach us the runes." *The Heliand, the Saxon Gospel,* Appendix 3, "Magic in the *Heliand,*" p. 215.

the runes in the fuþark, no matter how wrong it was in detail and misguided in literal method, was in a sense prescient. He was the first to suggest that the sequence of the runes might in some way point to words. He maintained that "father" was the first word indicated, and he detected the Christian echo, but did not perceive the pagan-Christian ambiguity. He never realized that the rune sequence in the fuþark might be a mnemonic line based on Germanic myth. My suggestion is that the elder fuþark is a sophisticated fourth-century mnemonic "alphabet," part of which can be read in two ways. In the syncretistic spirit of late antiquity, it made a distinct, if discrete, bow to the Christ of the Greeks, while telling the rune learner the traditional Germanic story of the origin of the norn-carved, talking twigs of Yggdrasil as an ancient gift to mankind from the All-father.

· and Christ are one ·
Father · and hallowed be he · long ago gave mankind talking staves as hereditary property.

ᚠᚢᚦᚨᚱ · ᚲ ᚷᚹ ᚺᚾ · ᛁ ᛃᛇᛈ ᛉ ᛊᛏᛒᛖ ᛗᛚᛜ ᛟᛞ

PART III

IN YULETIDE CAROL AND EVERGREENS

Chapter 7

Yggdrasil and the Christmas Tree

At Christmas time or at Yuletide, the wreath, the holly, and above all the Christmas tree, bring this long, intertwined, and evergreen tradition home to us across the centuries.

Some say, however, that the Christmas tree is exclusively pagan, and therefore has no place whatsoever in a Christian household, much less in a church.[1] Some claim the opposite, that the Christmas tree is a purely Christian German invention of the sixteenth century, with no possible paganism attached.[2] Against this, there is the point of view that we have seen held by the builders of the stave church and round church, by the sculptors of the Middleton Viking crosses and the baptismal font of Aakirkeby, perhaps even by the creator of the rune sequence of the fuþark, and by the bilingual sculptor of the Ruthwell cross and the poet of the *Dream of the Rood.* These artists suggest to both sides that they realize something about religion and

1. Not just the Christmas tree, but the entire celebration of Christmas was outlawed by the Puritans in England in 1642, and in 1647 with legal penalties by act of Parliament, until the Restoration in 1660. In New England, Calvinist antipathy to Christmas lasted into the mid-nineteenth century. See Francis X. Weiser, *The Christmas Book* (New York: Harcourt, Brace, 1952), pp. 43–49.
2. Weiser, *The Christmas Book*, p. 12. This is also Weiser's own opinion: "[The Christmas tree] is completely Christian in origin, and historians have never been able to connect it in any way with ancient Germanic or Asiatic mythology." Correspondingly, he restricts his notion of the original Christmas tree to the lighted and decorated versions of the sixteenth–seventeenth centuries.

language: in different religions there can be a confluence of things hoped for,[3] and in different religious languages there can be mutual comprehension and translation. People of good will can hear God speaking to them in biblical terms as did the shepherds in the fields of Bethlehem; or they can hear him as did the Magi, speaking to them in the language of the stars of the sky. As the international crowd at Pentecost remarked in amazement, "We hear them declaring the wonders of God in our own tongues."[4] In the Christmas tree just such a beautiful mutuality-in-diversity stands its ground against the winter cold.

And so, before attempting to trace something of the beginnings of the Christmas tree, it might be good to take a look first at the word for the Christmas season in the North, Yule. Except for the occasional romantic use of "Yuletide," this is no longer a very common expression outside the Scandinavian lands. It is however a significant word and I would suggest it has a possible connection to one of the other most popular of the Christmas decorations: the evergreen wreath.

THE WREATH

Like most Yule/Christmas artifacts, the evergreen wreath and tree have long and deep roots extending back to distant times that are enshrouded in myth, legend, and, thankfully, carol. They point to a celebration of a crucial and recurrent time of the year that is, even if less realized, as pivotal now as it was in those agrarian ages. The meaning of the word Yule can help show the path back. The earliest author describing the calendar use of Yule is the Venerable Bede (d. 735). In his commentary on the times of the year *De Temporum*

3. Heb. 11:1–2.
4. Acts 2:11.

Ratione[5] he describes his Anglian, non-Christian contemporaries' method of the calculating the passage of time—it is done by the moon. He says they call *luna* "mona" [moon] and from that they get "monath" [month]. Important for our purposes is that Bede writes that they call both of the months of December and January by the same name "Guli" [Yule], and he continues that "the night that is now so holy to us is called by them in the vernacular Modranicht, *id est matrum noctem* [that is, the Night of the Mothers]" because, he suspects, of "the ceremonies they perform as they observe a vigil all night [*pervigilantes*]"—presumably in their honor.

Two items here are of importance to us. "Their New Year," Bede writes, "begins with the night when we celebrate the Birth of the Lord. This very night that is now so holy to us, the night of Christmas, or Christmas Eve, is to them 'Modranicht, *id est matrum noctem*' and is celebrated with an all-night vigil kept in honor of the "Mothers" maternal function in giving birth to what child or children?". Since this is the night of the winter solstice, and the beginning of the New Year, "the Mothers," I suspect, is another term for the women who attend to the tree of the universe over the course of time.[6] They are the ones who know and write the runes of time; whose three names, What Happened, What Is Happening, and What Shall Happen, indicate the forward movement of fate and time: they are the Norns.

5. Patrologia Latina, 90 (De Mensibus Anglorum), p. 356. The paraphrase/translation of the text in the following lines is mine.
6. Another opinion is that the Anglians' "Mothers Eve" festival is in honor of the Roman-Germanic-Celtic *Matronae*, "great mothers," or "matrons," deities honored especially in the lower Rhineland, and related to the dead. The Angles and Saxons, however, seem to have associated their *matres*, "mothers," with the three Norns, with time as turning the wheel of the new year. The many *matronae*, though often also depicted as a seated group of three, were not particularly honored on the eve of Yule, which, as Bede describes, the Anglians' *matres* clearly were. In addition, Saxo Grammaticus (*Gesta Danorum* VI, 181) years later, also associates the matrons with the parcae. For discussion see Rudolf Simek, *Dictionary of Northern Mythology* (Cambridge: D. S. Brewer, 1993), pp. 204–8.

The eve of December 25[7] must have been their maternal "feast day." On December 25 they become (to answer Bede) mothers of a new era of time; their child, a New Year, is born. The Angles must also have made sacrifice to them in some way or performed rituals which Bede either knows and does not wish to mention, or of which he is unaware.[8] His description is enough to let the reader know that this is a very important feast of the passage of time. Whatever the Angles did, it must have been to show honor and reverence to the "Mothers" in their function of watering and loaming Yggdrasil the tree that supports all life, in the hope that the Norns will also be favorable to their lives and to the life of the sun as it struggles with cold and darkness to execute the turn in its course which begins the New Year.

The other item is on the calendric nature of Yule itself. For the Angles, Yule consists of the month of December, when the south-moving sun slows to a stop and a new year begins, and of January as the sun slowly begins moving northward. Yule is primarily the night of December, December 24, and then includes the twelve days following. In other words, Yule proper consists of a twelve-day celebration embedded in the middle of two full months, all called Yule. December is called ærra geola, or "Fore-Yule," and January is called, with Germanic consistency, æftera geola, or "After-Yule." And the twelve days which they surround are simply "Yule" itself.

7. This was the solstice eve in Bede's time. Nowadays it is actually December 21, though Christmas will no doubt be kept on the December 25 for some centuries; and the equinox is now September 21.

8. Whatever it was that was going on during Bede's New Year's Eve vigil was still going on three hundred years later, and at Worcester and York. Wulfstan, bishop of Worcester, in his *Canons* (c.1006), moreover, is as quiet as Bede about specifics when he urges his priests to "extinguish every heathen practice," including "the devil's work of drawing children through the earth, and the nonsense that is performed on Years Eve [*on geares niht*] in various kinds of sorcery at *friðsplottum* [peace-places; grave sites?] and at elder trees." Cited in Della Hook's study, *Trees in Anglo-Saxon England: Literature, Lore and Landscape* (Woodbridge, Suffolk: The Boydell Press, 2010), pp. 31–32 [transl. modified].

Though Eastern Mediterranean peoples may have chosen to prefer the first month of spring when the sun entered Aries and the sheep bore lambs to celebrate the New Year, they lived in a far more moderate climate. Between the fiftieth parallel of latitude and the Arctic Circle, a whole different snow-filled concept of winter exists, not only one colder, darker, and of longer duration, but one that can be and was far more threatening to life. In the North, as summer wears on, the farmer can watch the sun on the eastern horizon rising each day a little bit farther south of a hill or rock used as a marker on the horizon-line. Each succeeding day it crosses the sky at a continuously lower angle so that even at midday by October it stands low in the sky. No one can fail to see that trees and bushes cast longer and darker shadows. The sun no longer rises in the exact east, at 90° on the compass, as it does on the equinox on September 25,[9] but at 55° north latitude, the approximate latitude of Bornholm, Oslo (60°), and Copenhagen; on December 25 the sun rises much farther to the south, at 135° on the compass, the point of southeast.[10] During the time between September and December the point of sunrise moves a full 45 degrees along the horizon, an enormous distance clearly visible in terms of the hills and farms on the horizon. The sun also sets correspondingly farther south in the west, and travels in a low arc across the daytime sky, bringing increasing cold and gradually predominant darkness. This being a natural celestial movement, it is totally beyond human

9. As it was in medieval times. Due to precession, the 26,000-year wobble of the earth's tilted axis, the date is now the 21st of September. It is, however, the mono-directional steadiness of the 23 degree tilt of the earth's rotational axis, when it points away from the sun in December, January, and February, that causes the severity of winter in the upper latitudes of the North, and the apparent movement and wheeling of the sun on the horizon.

10. Above 66° latitude, in northern Norway above Trondheim (63°), the sun does not rise at all above the horizon on December 25 [old calendar]—that must have been genuinely, if regularly, frightening and called even more for maintaining trust in the evergreen. I am indebted for the above calculations to a friend, Prof. Raymond J. Pfeiffer, professor of astronomy and physics at Trenton State University.

control and beyond control of the gods. It is thus no wonder that resort was made to natural prayer and natural magic to attempt to help the sun from being dragged downward by the forces of cold and night. For life to continue, the sun had to be encouraged to halt its southern drive, to use its strength to stop, to turn itself around and wheel toward the north. In the South, what was important was that the sun stop its retreat—thus the Latin word, *solstice*: sol-*stasis*—that the sun stand still. In the frozen North, far more imperative than stopping was that the sun then re-*turn*. This I believe is the origin of the Yule wreath.

The wreath is a solar wheel, made of evergreen branches, celebrating the day, December 25, (nowadays, December 21) when the sun finally stops its southern movement into darkness, reaches its pivot point and over the next twelve days, wheels around and slowly begins northward movement in its daily rising. Life can be reassured; light and heat will return. The evergreen, from the holly to the ivy, the spruce to the laurel, have been shown to be right in their constancy and hope that life will return. Ragnarok, when the sun will be devoured by the wolf of darkness, and its fearful precursor, the time when the devastating *fimbul*-winter of three years' duration will come upon Middlegard, is not at hand. Instead, once again, the sun will slowly wheel, turning back north.

It has been suggested that the ultimate origin of the word Yule is related to the English word *wheel*, "in which case it would denote etymologically the 'turn' of the year."[11] (See Figure 7.1.) The

11. John Ayto, *Dictionary of Word Origins* (New York: Arcade [Little, Brown, & Co.], 1990), p. 582. Ayto favors the suggestion of an ultimate Indo-European origin for Yule as **qwelo [or kwelo],* meaning "go round." I agree. The *OED* stops at pre-Germanic, giving the origin of the word as obscure; modern Danish, however, still has *hjul* for "wheel" [and *jul* for Christmas].

Jan de Vries also gives the Greek *kyklos* [cycle, turning] as a possible correlative for yule and postulates an indo-germanic *jekylom as the "turning pole" and thus arrives at *deichselwendung des sonnenwagens,* the turning around of the pulling shaft of the solar wagon, a rather more picturesque vision of the root for yule. *Altnordisches etymologisches Wörterbuch* (Leiden: Brill, 1962), p. 292.

Figure 7.1. Bronze age carved boulder on Bornholm depicting schematically an expedition of ten ships either returning from (or heading out to) the sea. The two solar wheels are at the left hand edge, possibly indicating a journey of two yules' time. Author's photograph.

Germanic word for turning around, for turning on a pivot, or wheeling, is "Yule." Thus, as Bede reported, this is an important moment in the North. Two full months point forward and back to the time of the turn, Fore Yule and After Yule, or: Forewheel and Afterwheel, and the feast itself is met with an all night vigil and twelve days of feasting and celebration—and with bringing the hope-filled and prophetic evergreens inside the house and hall. The evergreens profess by their greenness and stability nature's confidence that life will return once again this year. A most appropriate shape for these evergreens must have been the "wheel"[12] made from twisting and plaiting evergreen branches into the shape of the wheel, the "Yule" that the sun was at the moment performing and which the evergreens predicted.

It is easy to see how this wreath symbolism and hope could have been seen by northern Christians as having been fulfilled by the birth of Christ. He is presented as the light of the world in the Gospel of John, and his coming brings light to the world and illuminates the darkness like the returning sun. His nativity initiates a turn into a new era, a New Year that will never end. Without any change, the wreath alone could be seen as a northern prediction of the coming of light, its circular shape suggests the movement of God coming north, and circular composition of evergreens suggests life that will not end. If laurel is used, then the wreath even stands in harmony with the laurel wreaths of victory used in the South to honor the Unconquered Sun, *Sol Invictus,* at this time of the year. Placed on the door and hanging in the halls of the Anglo-Saxon north, its merry greenness offers a welcome to the stranger to come in out of the cold and join the festivities.

The Yule wreath was eventually Christianized further by the addition of lights. This appears to have happened in Germany in the sixteenth century[13] with the creation of the Advent wreath out of

12. In the sunny and more equatorial Mediterranean, as in Egypt, the sun is often depicted as seen on the horizon: a radiant disk. In the North, where clouds and solar north-south movement have profound effects, and where the winter Yule-turn is more vital, the sun is depicted as a wheel with four spokes. The archaeological solar wheel petrographs carved above boats (as on Bornholm) may be prayers for good weather, but may also, I suggest, indicate the number of (new) years, Yules, that an expedition took.
13. See Weiser, *Handbook of Christian Feasts and Customs,* pp. 54–55.

the Yule wreath. The Advent season occupies most of what would have been called the month of Fore-Yule in any case, and would have been seen as natural to have a "Fore-Christmas" month as well. The Advent wreath has four candles in its ring, one is lighted each week of Advent in honor, as is told, of the 4,000 years that the Jews waited for the coming of the light. Finally on Christmas Eve, with all four candles burning, a large white candle is found shining brightly at the crossing of the wheel in the middle of the evergreen circle. The whole advent wreath is suspended from the ceiling, and turns, moving gently in the breeze, as though it were marking the passage of time, moving slowly like the sun on the horizon, until the dark evening of the 24th of December, when the Yule wreath's perpetual hope is fulfilled at Christmastide. The child who is the light of the world has arrived to become the radiant, white center candle at the intersection of the spokes of the evergreen wheel.

THE CHRISTMAS TREE

It is hard for me to imagine Christmas without two things: the tree and the music. The tree's coming into the house, reversing the natural order of things, and standing majestically in a corner of the living room instead of being outside in the forest, never struck me as strange, quite the opposite, it filled me with awe. The tree in the room whispered happiness is here, spiritually and naturally, "and heav'n and nature sing."

As the tree stands in the corner sending its forest aroma of pine throughout the house and season, the time is filled with the happiness of children and adults celebrating the birth of the Savior. The music of Handel's *Messiah* brings the other live great presence of Christmas into the house: the prophet Isaiah.

For unto us a Child is born,
unto us a son is given,
And the government shall be upon his shoulder.
And his name shall be callèd:
Wonderful, counselor, the mighty God,
The everlasting Father, the Prince of Peace.[14]

The two prophetic traditions, Isaiah and Yggdrasil, stand together at Christmas time like David and the Sibyl,[15] proudly foretelling the birth of the savior of life. Isaiah with his ox and ass who know their master's manger[16] has also spoken through almost every painter who has depicted the nativity scene. In the northern tradition it is the silent but eloquent and persistent voice of the evergreen tree, Yggdrasil, whose winter tale begins with the three years of uninterrupted winter snowfall, continues with the violent collapse of the entire world, and ends with the miraculous prophesy in which Life and Lifthrasir emerge from the protection of the evergreen's tree trunk, that speaks to all. What other tale could the evergreen tree be imagined to tell but that of salvation from the snow and ice and the reemergence of the green of life from a very long winter?

Early English Christmas carols also give witness to the presence of the evergreen tree inside the hall, telling its tale of hope. There is a series of carols on the theme of the holly and the ivy which both suggest the relative situation of the two evergreens in the wild, and allude to the rivalry of man (the holly) and woman (the ivy).[17] The lyrics are good natured and assume the rivalry of fans of the holly

14. Is. 9: 6.
15. As in the third line of the medieval poem *Dies Irae* (c.1250). The stanza avers that the coming of doomsday is prophesied both by the Old Testament and by the Roman Sibylline Books: *teste David cum Sibylla* [*both David and the Sibyl give witness*].
16. Is. 1:3.
17. Richard Leighton Greene, *The Early English Carols*, 2nd ed., carols 136–139.1 (Oxford: Clarendon, 1977), pp. 82–83.

and of fans of the ivy, and are designed it seems to be danced by men and women in a circle dance, perhaps in the lord's or local chieftain's hall. In England the holly, rather than the spruce or pine, seems to have been the preferred evergreen tree for Yuletide celebrations and would have had the place of honor in the hall, perhaps with the wassail bowl before it and the blazing Yule log behind. The following first lines are excerpted from two carols in a fifteenth- and sixteenth-century manuscript, modernized by the author:

Nay, Ivy, nay, it shall not be as you wish;
Let Holly have the mastery, as the custom is.
*
Holly stood in the hall, fayre to behold;
Ivy stood outside the door; she is full sore a-cold.
Holly and his merry men, they're dancing and they sing;
Ivy and her maidens, they're weeping and [their hands] they wring.
*
Holly bears red berries, and plenty of them too,
The thristlecock, the popyngay, dance on every bough.
Well now, poor Ivy, what birds have you
Except the poor little owlet that sings "hoo, hoo?"
*
Ivy bears berries as black as any sloe;
The wood-pigeon comes and feeds on them,
She lifts up her tail and shits before she goes—
Not for a hundred pounds would she
Treat the Holly so.[18]

18. For the originals, see Greene, *The Early English Carols*, p. 82. Greene also finds that especially the second version above suggests the connection to the traditional "The Holly and the Ivy," whose stanzas begin with the line familiar from above: "The holly bears a berry." The traditional "The Holy and the Ivy" was first printed in a broadside around 1710, but derives, as can be seen in the above, from much earlier sources (p. 382).

Greene makes the comment that the first comes from an older text, which would put the song back to the high Middle Ages and its continuing merriment over the winter solstice. Several other of these carols praise the ivy as the champion at defeating the winter weather by staying green in the cold and even for use as medicine.[19] In none of these songs is there as yet a Christmas treatment of the evergreen theme, but in one traditional carol that is derived from the late medieval holly and ivy carols we can see a parallel process to that of the Yule wreath becoming the Christmas wreath, namely, and appropriately, "The Holly and the Ivy." This carol's Welsh version and melody was first published in 1710 and was later published as a folklore find in 1910 by Cecil Sharp from oral sources based on a usage at Sans parish in Cornwall. Cecil Sharp was a collector and preserver of folklore, famous for his rescue of morris dancing and Yorkshire sword dancing from near extinction in England. His journey as a collector even brought him to the Appalachians looking for old folk-ballads.

The author of the lyrics is as obscure as the circumstances of composition, but as Greene commented, the verses about the berries show a very old connection leading back all the way to the holly and ivy contest songs of the late middle ages. The old contest shows up in the first stanza, and the refrain again and again suggests a Yuletide merriment equally old: the rising of the sun, now happily mixed with the music of Christmas.

The holly and the ivy,
When they are both full grown
Of all the trees that are in the wood

19. Greene, p. 84, "Ivy is both fair and gre[e]n,/In wynter and in somer also,/And it is medecinable, I wen [think],/Who knew the vertus that [be-]long thereto;/Ivy,/It is good and lusty/And in its kynd a wel go[o]d tre[e]."

The holly bears the crown.
O the rising of the sun
And the running of the deer
The playing of the merry organ
Sweet singing in the choir.

[The Christianization of the evergreen tree takes the form of a comparison of the small white flower of the holly to the innocence and lack of showiness of the birth of Christ as baby:]

The holly bears a blossom as white as lily flower
And Mary bore sweet Jesus Christ
To be our sweet Savior.
O the rising of the sun
And the running of the deer. . . .

[The constant repetition of the rising of the sun in the refrain, causes listener and singer in the choir to weave back and forth associating the meaning of the rising of the midwinter sun and the wheeling of the sun to return north, first with the birth and then with the passion of Christ (in the following stanzas).]

The holly bears a berry
As red as any blood
And Mary bore sweet Jesus Christ
To do poor sinners good.
O the rising of the sun
And the running of the deer. . . .

[In the older versions of the holly-ivy theme, the redness of the berry was seen as a decided contrast to the black berries of the ivy;

now the red color of the holly's berry is associated with Christ's bleeding, and the blood on the cross with the berries on the tree. The holly tree is being identified with the cross, the tree of the Crucifixion, almost as if it could speak as in *The Dream of the Rood.* The refrain in this context serves as a contrasting and encouraging reminder of the "rising of the sun" that will occur after the Crucifixion.]

> The holly bears a prickle
> As sharp as any thorn;
> And Mary bore sweet Jesus Christ
> On Christmas Day in the morn.
> O the rising of the sun
> And the running of the deer. . . .

[The sharp prickles at the end of the holly leaf are a reminder of the crown of thorns, as is immediately clear, and the almost fatalistic mention of Christ's death on this day suggests that he too will have to go to meet whatever dark fate the Norns have spun for him. This is a nice juxtaposition, and is touchingly trailed by the refrain, promising that his fate will not be his end. He will rise like the sun and life will rejoice like the running of the deer.]

> The holly bears a bark
> As bitter as any gall;
> And Mary bore sweet Jesus Christ
> For to redeem us all.
> O the rising of the sun
> And the running of the deer. . . .

[As Jesus had to drink the wine mixed with gall that the soldiers reached up him on a sponge as he hung on the cross, the holly has bark that can also be used to create a bitter drink, echoing as well the bitter drink Christ asked to be spared in the agony in the garden. Possibly the bitter drink may perhaps allude to the medicinal use of holly mentioned in the carol above. In any case, Jesus's drinking of the bitterness of the passion and death became the medicine "for to redeem us all."]

The holly and the ivy
Now both are well grown,
Of all the trees that are in the wood,
The holly bears the crown.

[Now that the evergreen tree has come fully into its own, bearing the marks of the passion of Christ as a tree once bore Christ himself. Like the tree in *The Dream of the Rood,* the tree can now be called full grown, that is, having become the fulfillment of the hope promised by its branches, by the story of its ever-green leaves, its refusal to be defeated by the white death of winter. In a subtly evocative line in the refrain, the evergreen tree is associated with the deer, and thus with Yggdrasil, whose branches can be relied on to provide food for the deer that have to nibble at its branches during the winter. Like Isaiah, the holly serves as a prophet predicting what the suffering servant, once born, would have to endure in dying. Like the wreath, the holly tree identifies the death of Christ as being like one of its own winters, a Yule. He, like an evergreen tree will persist; like the sun, he will wheel, rise, re-turn, to run with the deer in winter while choirs and angels sing.]

O the rising of the sun
And the running of the deer

The playing of the merry organ
Sweet singing in the choir.[20]

The evergreen tree standing in the hall is already recognized in "The Holly and the Ivy" as the Christmas tree, or the "Christ tree," the *Christbaum,* as is said in Germany, related to salvation even before the addition of the traditional decoration and lights. It therefore seems much too restrictive to me to consider the first Christmas tree to come into existence only when ornaments were used to establish a biblical identity for the evergreen as the tree of temptation in the Garden of Paradise. Indeed we need only recall the letter of Pope Gregory the Great to the Abbot Mellitus (which we saw in connection with the stave churches), to recall that Gregory wanted not only the "well-made" pagan temples to remain, minus their gods, but to be used for Christian worship. It is not often considered that he also had a concern that pagan feasts and feasting be retained, also no doubt minus their attendant gods. I am sure the natural religious feast of the Yule turning of the year, and its "well-made" symbols of the Yule wreath and the Yule evergreen tree, also fit under his category of good things to retain from the old religion.

There is even an old etiological legend that gives a justification for distinguishing between the tree worship of Thor's oak for example, and reverence for the pine tree. The legend adds to the story of the event when St. Boniface, following Charlemagne's example with the Irminsul, marched with Frankish soldiers to Geismar. There he

20. Some believe the deer are a memory of the hunting necessary for the Yule feast. Others think that especially the last two lines of the refrain mentioning organ and choir may have been added by the publisher of the broadside, the first stanza possibly being an earlier refrain. For discussion, see *The New Oxford Book of Carols,* edited by HughKeyte and Andrew Parrott, assisted by Clifford Bartlett (Oxford/New York: Oxford University Press, 1992), pp. 436–37. The editors believe the carol certainly antedates the publication of the broadside: "a much earlier origin (for the verses at least) seems likely, particularly since so many medieval 'holly and ivy' songs and carols are known."

found the sacred oak of Thor and ordered the native Saxon pagans to be assembled so they could watch as he, backed by the soldiers, chopped it down in front of them.[21] The legend adds a miraculous event to this chronicle version. As retold by Jonathan Greene: after the tree had fallen Boniface looked down and saw that "from the roots of the felled oak a fir tree was growing. To his holy eyes the fir was a symbol of Christ's resurrection, with new life growing out of what had been a tree of death."[22] This legend seems to have as its purpose to take away any qualms about having evergreens in the house as being paganism. Instead, the story gives a Christian justification for showing reverence to the evergreen tree by associating it with St. Boniface himself in his most famous act of destroying a pagan tree, and associates the pine with continuing life and resurrection. The legend also disassociates the fir from the indiscriminate hanging of human beings and animals as sacrifices on trees as reported by Adam of Bremen, who was relating what he had been told of the sacred oak at Upsala.[23] It is quite clear in any case that the thinner and densely grouped branches of a pine or spruce are really not at all as appropriate for sustaining multiple hangings as are those of the mighty oak. Mythologically, the story is also interesting because it both associates the new religion with the old, and shows a new tree purified of the oak's use for death sentences. The evergreen tree can stand for life in both religions; under a more benevolent Christianity it is seen as emerging from the roots of the fallen oak. This story must be associated with those Christians who were inculturating their faith, adapting to the local Germanic religious

21. See Murphy, *The Saxon Savior, The Germanic Transformation of the Gospel in the Ninth-Century* Heliand, pp. 13–15.

22. Jonathan Green, *A Christmas Miscellany* (Skyhorse Publishing, 2009), p. 29. There are also other versions of the story in one of which Boniface notices that the oak as it fell destroyed all the trees in its path with the exception of a small pine tree.

23. *The Heliand, The Saxon Gospel*, pp. 199–200.

customs and iconography, treating the evergreen as prophetic, and building stave and round churches. The tale helps make it appropriate for Christians to have an evergreen tree, pine or holly, in their hall as they celebrate Christ's birth.

Other medieval legends show the growing acceptance of the role of the tree as part of the nativity of Christ by imagining a reverential role for the tree in the Christmas narrative and beyond. Perhaps the most impressive are the tales of the bowing of the tree or trees to Christ and his mother. Even if human beings did not always recognize who he was, the trees knew, and realized who was passing by, so say the stories. We have already seen this in the efforts of the tree to bow down in *The Dream of the Rood,* when it realized it had to stay upright with its burden. In the nativity story it is the flight into Egypt which gives the poets the imaginative opportunity to bewail human unawareness of divine presence by contrasting it with the perceptive awareness of the trees by the side of the road. In *The Golden Legend* (c. 1260), Jacobus de Voragine gives an example of a tree that was itself already very well gifted with almost magical curative ability, immediately recognizing the divine source of its tree-power:

> And Cassiodorus tells us in his *Tripartite History* that in Hermopolis in the Thebaid there is a tree called *persidis,* which cures any sickness if one of its fruits, or a leaf, or a piece of its bark is applied to the neck of the sick person. When blessed Mary fled into Egypt with her Son, this tree bent down to the ground and adored the Christ.[24]

As in the case of the beginning of Isaiah, we feel rebuked that not only do the ox and the ass know their master's stall, but even the tree. . . .

24. Jacobus de Voragine, *The Golden Legend, Readings on the Saints,* vol. 1, William Granger Ryan, trans. (Princeton, NJ: Princeton University Press), p. 57.

Another legend that bears clear markings of being influenced by the myth of Yggdrasil as protector is the following one that again justifies the use of a pine tree. When the holy family was on the road fleeing from the soldiers of Herod and trying to reach the safety of Egypt, many plants offered them shelter. When Mary was too weary to travel any longer, the family stopped at the edge of a forest to rest. A gnarled and withered old pine tree that had grown hollow from its years invited Mary and Joseph and the child to rest within its trunk. When the holy family did so, the branches closed around them and hid them from the soldiers who were searching for them. When the soldiers had passed the holy family left, and when they did, the Christ child turned and blessed the pine tree, and the imprint of the infant Jesus's hand was left forever within the fruit of the tree, the pine cone.[25]

It is hard to miss that this tale is a version of the protective function of Yggdrasil in hiding the Lif and Lifthrasir in its trunk as the deadly horrors of Ragnarok approach, and then setting them on their way again.

Other carols also sang of the cherry tree bowing so that Mary, pregnant, could have some of its fruit to eat, despite the angry Joseph; or paintings show the trees by the road bowing as the holy family makes its way into Egypt. Perhaps one of the most touching of all these depictions of the tree bowing is the sculpture on the great stones at Externsteine in Germany. (See Figure 7.2.) The sculptor has depicted the descent from the cross and the harrowing of hell in a most unusual form—together. In the center, the dead Jesus, also completely bent over, is being handed down from the cross. Joseph of Arimathea is on the ground very reverently receiving the slumped body of his Lord onto his shoulder.

25. The pine cone has to be cut lengthwise to see this. Taken from the web, http://www.catholicdoors.com/misc/christmastree.htm.

Figure 7.2. The descent from the cross at Externsteine in Germany. A beautifully complex if much eroded depiction of the descent from the cross combined with the harrowing of hell and the Resurrection. All creation weeps, as it once almost did for Balder, as the sun and the moon above hide their faces in mourning cloths. Mary and John have been displaced to the left and right as the focus shifts to the figure of Joseph of Arimathea with the body of Christ bent over his shoulder. Nicodemus leans in sorrow and exhaustion on the cross while standing on the "great pillar," the Irminsul that represents Yggdrasil, as it bows to the ground, enabling Nicodemus to reach the crossbar and lower the body of Christ onto Joseph. There is no ladder in this version of the descent. The pillar of Yggdrasil, echoing the wish of the Rood, bows down, and becomes the ladder, so that Nicodemus can reach up and put his one arm around the cross while lowering the body of Christ to Joseph with the other. Down below, underneath the earth line, just below the conjoined bases of the Irminsul and the cross, the Nidhogg serpent is releasing its grip on the kneeling figures as it flees off to the right. Meanwhile Christ rises invisibly above the scene, blessing all. Drawing and partial restoration by Laurence Selim.

At the top, Nicodemus is holding on to the top of the cross with one arm around the crossbeam and with the other he is handing the body of Jesus down to Joseph of Arimathea. He is not standing on the ladder that is traditionally present in this scene. He is up by the crossbeam because the Irminsul, the great pillar that is the representation of Yggdrasil, has bent itself down to the ground to let Joseph use its back as a support to stand on. In inclining itself for this beautiful service, like the disciples in the scene and like Jesus himself, the Iminsul, Yggdrasil, is rendering loving service to its dead Lord; the tree trunk graciously acknowledging the cross. Down below the joined bases of the cross and the tree, below a line clearly marking the surface of the earth, just where the myth of Yggdrasil would predict it, there is an enormous underground dragonlike serpent. His head at the right end is hissing or roaring, while in the middle he holds a kneeling man and a woman in his coils. From the Edda we know what this creature is. It is the Nidhogg, and at this moment it is unwinding, releasing Adam and Eve from its coils, as it stretches out to flee to the right. Up above, as Christ rises with a blessing on the left, an exhausted looking Nicodemus on the right is a paradigm for the northern Christian: standing on Yggdrasil, he is able to get his arm around the cross.

The next phase in the development of the Christmas tree consists of the attachment of ornaments as a part of bringing the evergreen into closer visual association with the biblical tree. In the Garden of Paradise there were four trees, two of which were prohibited to Adam and Eve, the tree of life and the tree of the knowledge of good and evil. Adam and Eve fell to the snake's temptation to eat the fruit of the tree of knowledge of good and evil, and were expelled from the Garden of Eden and, as just seen, subjected to mortality.[26] The angel with the flaming sword was placed at the gate for fear they would come back

26. Gen. 2:8–3:24.

and "take also from the tree of life and eat, and live forever."[27] In the Middle Ages, the fall of Adam was a common subject for mystery play cycles, in England and in Germany. They were produced in England on the feasts of Corpus Christi and Pentecost and in Germany also during advent where the fall of Adam was seen as a good preparation for the coming of the Savior. Whether staged or produced on moving wagons called "pageants," or on temporary stages in front of the church, the one prop that the scene in the garden would have to have was the tree. It is not certain whether these trees were real or creations of the carpenters guild, the favorite, however, seems to have been the apple tree. This probably due to the (Latin) pun one can make on one of the two words[28] for apple: *malum. Malum* means apple, and also "evil." If the tree were a real one, and the play produced in December, the tree would have to have been a fir or holly, but there does not seem to be much evidence. David Bevington comments, "The tree must be an actual stage structure. At Norwich, such a tree was elaborately festooned with fruit and flowers of various descriptions. Iconographical tradition also sometimes represented the tree in such a way as to suggest the cross of the Crucifixion."[29]

In the Wakefield mystery play on the fall, *The Creation,* there is no description of the tree except that it is called the tree of life. There is however an elaborate description of what is on the tree:

". . . a house of Waynscott paynted and builded on a Cart with fowre wheels. . . . The tree displayed a wide variety of fruit and flowers: apples and figs, oranges, dates, almonds, colored thread to bind the flowers . . . a Rybbe colleryd Red."[30] The tree would defy biological

27. Gen 3:22.

28. The other word is *pomum,* which is also used but has no such double meaning.

29. David Bevington, *Medieval Drama* (Boston: Houghton Mifflin, 1975), p. 267.

30. *The Wakefield Mystery Plays,* Martial Rose, ed. (London: Evans Brothers, 1961), pp. 57–62, 85. The editor also notes that this tree may also have had to hold the two fig leaves. The "rybbe" colored red is perhaps in honor of the creation of Eve.

categorization as to origin just as much as Yggdrasil itself. On a more naturalistic stage one might expect two trees to represent the tree of life and the tree of the knowledge of good and evil, however on a moving cart this would be perhaps a bit too much tree, and in any case medieval poetic ingenuity enjoyed conflation. Because there is only one tree on the stage, it is the tree of life. Usually it is Satan who explains to Adam and Eve, and the audience, that the tree is the tree of life, but the fruit on the tree is where the forbidden knowledge of good and evil is found. Hence nicely explaining the poetic nature of the temptation, as having nothing to do with the tree, but with eating the fruit of the tree, and the elaborate and temptingly beautiful fruit and flowers on the tree. The number one fruit on the tree, however, because of the word play with *malum*, would most likely have been the apple.

An interesting illustration of this melding of the two trees can be seen in an illustration in 1481 by Berthold Furtmeyr for the missal of Archbishop Bernhard von Rohr of Salzburg. In the middle of the illustration is the tree of Eden hung with red apples and white oblata[31] (unconsecrated hosts). Adam is still asleep under the tree. On the right hand side of the tree Eve stands demure and naked, handing out apples from the tree to the kneeling faithful. On the left side of the tree a woman clothed in blue with a crown on her head, Mary, (or ecclesia) hands out white oblata from the tree to a further group of the kneeling faithful. Above Mary in the tree is a cross with Christ upon it, and above Eve there is a death's head looking down. In the middle wrapped around the tree trunk is the serpent who is kindly assisting Eve in the distribution of the apples.[32]

31. The frieze on the central pillar of the round church at Nylars, as mentioned carried the synthesis further: each individual apple in the tree is half white and half red with no white oblata.

32. http://www.leuninger-herbert.de/feste/07_Weihnacht/Brief.htm also in the Bayerische Staatsbibliothek München, Bernhard von Rohr, *Missale Quinque Tomis Constans,* Clm 15708–12. Image of the Tree in the missal is on line at this site.

The *Paradiesbaum*, as it was called in Germany, the tree of the Garden of Paradise came to be widely seen and known. It is Weiser's theory that the tree of paradise from the mystery plays (produced during advent in Germany) is the origin of the Christmas tree as we know it;[33] the tree came into the homes and halls of the faithful after, and because, the church discontinued the mystery plays when they became a bit too raucous. I doubt that all over the North evergreen trees would be suddenly brought into houses and halls to replace the tree of fruit and flowers that was the main prop of Adam and Eve plays. My theory is that the Christmas tree, like the wreath, is much older. It is the Yule evergreen tree, already standing for centuries in the snowbound winter hall. Thanks to the Adam and Eve plays, at this time it gradually came to be decorated with the apples and fruit of the tree of paradise, as it was associated with the Genesis story's tree of life. The apple tree was never brought into the house.[34] The evergreen came in long before the discontinuance of the mystery plays, and then seems to have been naturally receptive both to being conflated with the biblical tree of life, and to wearing the decorations and ornaments from the stage plays—and thus by the sixteenth century it became the Christmas tree as we know it.[35]

Perhaps not quite. There is now the question of candles and lights on the tree. Once again we are met with legend. Up until the middle of the seventeenth century, the Christmas tree had no candles on it, and in England at that time, as mentioned above, it

33. Weiser, *The Christmas Book*, 117–20.

34. There may be exceptions to this. In Bavaria a tree-shaped construction of apples and wooden dowels, wrapped in pine branches is set up at Christmas and is called a *Paradeis*. This custom seems to me to derive from the Christmas tree.

35. Weiser, *The Christmas Book*, gives mention made in Alsace in 1521 as first evidence for the transformation having occurred (pp. 119–20).

was not even permitted to exist. The Puritan regime outlawed celebration of Christmas in 1642 and enforced the prohibition later by penal law. This prohibition lasted until the restoration of the monarchy in1660, but held on in puritan New England, in Boston, until 1870. At the same time however, some Christmas customs continued on and even underwent expansion in Germany and the Nordic countries, and in England were revived after the Puritan era. Weiser believes the candles came to be transferred to the tree under the influence of two other Christmas artifacts, both of which had candles. One was the *Lichtstock*, or light stick, originally a candle on a wooden base that seems to have been a household, Christmastide version of the Easter season's paschal candle, and the other was the *Weichnachtspyramide*, the Christmas pyramid, a cone-shaped wooden pyramid, echoing the shape of the Christmas tree, set with candles at Christmas time.[36] Both of these candelabra may be folk derivations ultimately related to the liturgical use of candles: the *Lichtstock* to the Easter candle and the candles used on the altar during Mass; and in the case of the *Weihnachtspyramide*, to the triangular candelabra used during Benediction, or at vespers and compline during holy week. In any case, candles were transferred to the branches of the tree. The lighted Christmas tree then eventually made its way back to England a bit later thanks to Queen Victoria's love of Albert, who brought the custom with him from Germany. The Christmas tree returned to England shining brightly; it had become a candelabrum from nature.

The legendary answer to the question of the origin of the candles on the tree in Germany goes back to a story about Martin Luther. The story has no historical basis in Luther's life, but contains

36. Weiser, *The Christmas Book*, pp. 111–16, 119.

a surprising insight on the candles. As the legend is retold by Joseph Kelly:

> As the story goes, he [Luther] was going home on a clear winter evening and saw a fir tree covered by snow and with the bright stars behind it in the sky. Overcome by the beauty of the scene, he rushed home to tell his family. But he could not do so adequately, so he returned to the tree, cut it down, and brought it into his house. Naturally the snow melted quickly and the stars were outside, so Luther put candles on the tree to decorate it and to symbolize the stars with their light. This was the first Christmas tree in Germany.[37]

This is of course an etiological tale with an attributive fiction, a charming story aimed at explaining where things come from in an edifying, if a-historical, way. The legend aims at connecting the custom of bringing an evergreen tree into the house with someone of unimpeachable religious credentials and so to fend off any thought that bringing a tree into the house might possibly be a pagan custom with pre-christian roots. But the story has even more to say than that. Like the Boniface legend which associates the emerging pine with the fallen oak, this story implies an association of the candles on the tree with the stars in the sky. Thinking back both to the role of Yggdrasil as the support of the whole universe, whose branches contain all life forms and hold up the night sky, there is an ancient connection recognized here. Snorri wrote in *Gylfaginning* that Yggdrasil it the biggest and best of all trees. "Its branches spread out over all the world and extend across the sky."[38] And its enormous extent

37. Joseph F. Kelly, *The Feast of Christmas* (Collegeville, MN: Liturgical Press, 2010), p. 72.
38. Snorri, *Edda* (Everyman), p. 17.

can be caught partially by the eye when looking up in the winter night sky at the frosty Milky Way, the starry road between heaven and earth, the bifrost,[39] and being amazed as it glistens so brightly, uniting Asgard and Middlegard in Yggdrasil's branches. The legend of Luther's tree, perhaps without its creator's realizing it, holds resonances of a much older tale and serves to identify the Christmas tree with the tree whose branches align the stars of the night sky. The legend nicely presents this realization of the beauty of the tree and the stars as a new insight into the sanctity of nature itself as a saintly and Christian vision, but as we have seen, the insight is also a recovery in harmony with one quite old. The same insight is expressed particularly on the central pillar and the arched ceiling of the Olskirke on Bornholm. There the vines that emerge from the pillar and cover the whole ceiling are filled with the stars and constellations of the night sky. And in many other of the round churches, the incidents in Christ's life and death, his birth, Crucifixion, Resurrection as depicted on the central tree trunk are filled with vines and stars, as if to say it all of this happened here in our universe among the stars in the branches of Yggdrasil.

And so it would seem very appropriate in the Christmas tree's northern context to think of the candles on the branches of Yggdrasil as representing the stars, especially at the time of the very long darkness of the Yule and Christmas night sky. In a way they make the tree come alive to the eyes, shining with all the charm and magic that the world of natural creation already possesses—the Christmas tree

39. As we have seen above, there are two words for the bridge: *bilröst*, and especially in Snorri, *bifröst*. Scholars argue over whether the basic concept is that of the Milky Way, or of the rainbow. In my view it is a question of day and night visibility. In the daytime the high arc of the bridge can occasionally be glimpsed after a storm as the rainbow, and is called the *bilröst*; at night, and especially through most of the winter, the bridge can be seen as the high arching starry road of the Milky Way, the *bifröst*. (For discussion see John Lindow, *Norse Mythology*, pp. 80–81.)

reveals the whole of nature as a candelabrum whose candles are the stars. What then would be more appropriate for the top of the tree but a special star—like the white candle in the middle of the advent wreath—in honor of the Magi, those wise pagan foreigners, who like the Norse, found their way from their far-away country to the child with the help of their tales and their knowledge of the stars. They found him and left with evergreen branches of the tree of life in their hands. They had set out to find him with the help of their stories of Yggdrasil, which bent down, and upon which they, like Nicodemus, stood, and were supported so they could put their arm around the cross.

Where then should the traditional manger be placed? Where does it belong in this scheme of things? I can only answer that I believe the story of Yggdrasil suggests the most appropriate place. At the base of the Christmas tree, right in front of the trunk. Let the littlest members of the family be fascinated by crawling under the lowest branches of the tree, surrounded by pine needles and pine scent, with the magical many-colored glow of the tree lights warmly illuminating the little world, and there under the tree, let them find the child and his mother. At the very spot where, it is said, when the death of the world is over, God's tree will open its trunk, and out will come the life that was rescued, ready for a new year in a renewed world—Life and Lifthrasir. With these names the evergreen tree foretells the coming of the infant Jesus and the presence of Mary, it trembles, and ever smiles at Jesus held in a wooden crib.

SELECT BIBLIOGRAPHY

Agrell, Sigurd. "Die spätantike Alphabetmystik und die Runenreihe." In *Die spätantike alphabetmystik und die Runenreihe.* no. 6 (1931–1932): 155–210.

Anker, Peter, and Paul Hamlyn. *The Art of Scandinavia,* vol. 1. London and New York: Hamlyn, 1970. (Originally published in France by Zodiaque as *L'Art Scandinave I*, 1969.)

Anderson, Aron and Paul Hamlyn. *The Art of Scandinavia,* vol. 2. London and New York: Hamlyn, 1970. (Originally published in France by Zodiaque as *L'Art Scandinave* 2, 1968.)

Astell, Ann W. *Eating Beauty, The Eucharist and the Spiritual Arts of the Middle Ages.* Ithaca and London: Cornell University Press, 2006.

Bede, the Venerable. *Ecclesiastical History of the English People.* Translated by Leo Sherley-Price, revised by R. E. Latham. London: Penguin, 1990.

Berg, K. "The Gosforth Cross." In *Journal of the Warburg and Courtauld Institutes,* XXI (1958): 27–43.

Bertelsen, Lise Gjeddsø. "On Öpir's pictures." In *Runes and their Secrets: Studies in Runology*. Edited by Marie Stocklund et al. Copenhagen: Museum Tusculanum Press, University of Copenhagen, 2006.

Bugge, Anders. *Norwegian Stave Churches.* Translated by Ragnar Christophersen. Oslo: Dreyers Vorlag, 1953.

Byock, Jesse. "Sigurðr Fáfnisbani: An Eddic Hero Carved on Norwegian Stave Churches." In *Poetry in the Scandinavian Middle Ages. The Seventh International Saga Conference.* Edited by Theresa Pároli. Spoleto: Centro Italiano di Studi Sull'Alto Medioevo, 1990.

Christie, Sigrid and Hakon. *The Torpo Stave-Church.* Translated by Clifford Long. Oslo: The Society for the Preservation of Norwegian Ancient Monuments

(Fortidsminneforenigingen), 1999. [This society sponsors research and guide books with historical drawings and schematics as well as excellent photographs of the stave churches. It also sponsors students to act as guides during the summer.]

Corpus Christianorum, Series Latina, Bedae Venerabilis Opera, Pars VI: Opera Didascalia, vol. CXXVIIIB. Turnholt: Brills, 1977.

Crossland, R. W. and R.Hayes. "Bound Dragon Crosses at Middleton, Pickering." *Yorkshire Archaeological Journal*, 38 (1955): 453.

Crossley-Holland, Kevin. *The Norse Myths*. The Pantheon Fairy Tale and Folklore Library. New York: Pantheon Books, 1980.

Dahm, Murray. "Re-examining the Latin Cursive Elements in Fuþark Development." In *Amsterdamer Beiträge zur älteren Germanistik*, 55 (2002): 15–21.

Davidson, H. R. Ellis. *Gods and Myths of Northern Europe*. New York: Penguin, 1979.

———. *The Golden Age of Northumbria*. London: Longmans, Green & Co., 1958.

———. *Scandinavian Mythology*. London/New York: Hamlyn, 1969.

De Vries, Jan. *Altgermanische Religionsgeschichte*. Berlin: Walter de Gruyter, 1957.

———. *Altnordisches etymologisches Wörterbuch*. Leiden: Brill, 1962.

The Dream of the Rood. Edited by Bruce Dickens and Alan S. C. Ross. New York: Appleton Century Crofts, 1966.

The Dream of the Rood. Edited by Michael Swanton. Exeter: University of Exeter, 1987.

Düwel, Klaus. "Runeninschrift auf einem 'Schemel' aus einem Bootgrab bei Wremen. In *Nytt om runer* 9 (1994): 14–16.

———, and Wilhelm Heizmann. "Das ältere Fuþark: Überlieferung und Wirkungsmöglichkeiten." In *Das* fuþark – *Reallexikon der germanischen Altertumskunde*, Ergänzungsband 51, Berlin/New York: Walter de Gruyter, 2006, pp. 54–60.

———, and Wilhelm Heizmann. "Der Neufund des Runen-Braklteaten IK 585 Sankt Ibs Vej-C Roskilde (Zur Ikonologie der Goldbrakteaten, LXII)." In *Runica–Germanica – Mediaevalia*, Band 37. New York/Berlin: Walter de Gruyter, 2003, 243–64.

The Early English Carols, 2nd ed. Edited by Richard Leighton Greene. Oxford: Clarendon Press, 1977.

The Elder or Poetic Edda, Part One—The Mythological Poems. Edited and translated by Olive Bray. London, the King's Weighhouse Rooms: The Viking Club, 1908.

The Elder Edda, A Book of Viking Lore. Translated by Andy Orchard. London/New York: Penguin, 2011.

Farjon, Aljos. *A Natural History of Conifers*. Portland, OR: Timber Press, 2008.

Firby, M. and J. T. Lang, "The Pre-Conquest Sculptures at Stonegrave." In *The Yorkshire Archaeological Journal*, 53 (1981): 21–22.

Fletcher, Richard. *The Barbarian Conversion, From Paganism to Christianity*. Berkeley: University of California Press, 1997.

Fulton, Rachel. *From Judgment to Passion: Devotion to Christ and the Virgin Mary, 800–1200.* New York: Columbia University Press, 2002.

Gering, Hugo. *Vollständiges Wörterbuch zu den Liedern der Edda.* Halle: Verlag der Buchhandlung des Waisenhauses, 1903.

Grönvik, Ottar. "Über die Bildung des älteren und jüngeren Runenalphabets." In *Osloer Beiträge zur Germanistik,* Bd. 29. Edited by Ottar Grønvik. Frankfurt: Peter Lang, 2001: 52–54.

Hadley, Dawn. "Lordship and the Danelaw." In *Cultures in Contact, Scandinavian Settlement in England in the Ninth and Tenth Centuries.* Edited by Dawn M. Hadley and Julian D. Richards. Turnhout, Belgium: Brepols, 2000: 117ff.

Hagen, Anders. *The Viking Ship Finds.* Oslo: Universitets Oldsaksamling, 1967.

Hauck, Karl and Wilhelm Heizmann. "Der Neufund des Runen-Brakteaten IK 585 Sankt Ibs Vej-C Roskilde." In *Runica Germanica Mediaevalia,* Bd. 37 (*Reallexikon der germanischen Altertumskunde*). Edited by Wilhelm Heizmann. Berlin/New York: Walter de Gruyter, 2003: 244–64.

Heales, Alfred. *The Ecclesiology of Gottland, other than that of Wisby; and the Churches of Bornholm.* London, High Holborn: Roworth & Co., 1889.

Heliand und Genesis. Herausgegeben von. Otto Behaghel, bearbeitet von Burghard Taeger. Tübingen: Niemeyer, 1984.

Heliand, The Saxon Gospel. Translated with commentary by G. Ronald Murphy, S.J. New York and Oxford: Oxford University Press, 1992.

Høst, Oluf. *Bornholms Rundkirker, Tekst af Th. Lind.* Rønne: William Dams Forlag, 1964.

Hohler, Erla Bergendahl. "Stave Church," In *The Dictionary of Art, in 29 Volumes.* Edited by Jane Turner. London: Macmillan, 1986.

Hooke, Della. *Trees in Anglo-Saxon England.* Woodbridge, Suffolk: The Boydell Press, 2010.

Jacobsen, Torsten Cumberland. *The Gothic War: Rome's Final Conflict in the West.* Yardley, PA: Westholme Publishing, 2009.

Jensen, Hans. *Die Schrift in Vergangenheit und Gegenwart.* 2. neubearbeitete Auflage. Berlin: Deutscher Verlag der Wissenschaften, 1958.

Jesch, Jessica. *Vikings and Men in the Late Viking Age, The Vocabulary of Runic Inscriptions and Skaldic Verse.* Woodbridge, Suffolk/Rochester, NY: The Boydell Press, 2001.

Kelly, Joseph F. *The Feast of Christmas.* Collegeville, MN: Liturgical Press, 2010.

Kendall, Calvin B. "From Sign to Vision: The Ruthwell Cross and the *Dream of the Rood.*" In *The Place of the Cross in Anglo-Saxon England.* Edited by Catherine Karkov, Sarah Larratt Keefer, and Karen Louise Jolly. Woodbridge, Suffolk: The Boydell Press, 2006.

Kure, Henning. "Hanging on the World Tree: Man and Cosmos in Old Norse Mythic Poetry." In *Old Norse Religion in Long-Term Perspectives: Origins, Changes and Interactions.* Edited by Anders Andrén et al. Lund: Nordic Academic Press, 2007.

Kluge, Friedrich. "Runenschrift und Christentum." In *Germania: Korrespondenzblatt der Römisch-Germanischen Kommission des Kaiserlichen Archäologischen Instituts.* Herausgegeben vom deutschen archaeologischen Institut. Frankfurt: Jos. Baer & Co., 1919: 43–48.

Knirk, James E. "Runic Inscriptions containing Latin in Norway." In *Runeneinschriften als Quellen interdisziplinärer Forschung.* Ergänzungsbände zum Reallexikon der germanischen Altertumskunde 15. Edited by Klaus Düwel. Berlin: Hikuin, 1998.

Knudsen, Ann Vibeke. *The Old Churches of Bornholm.* Edited and text. Rønne, Bornholm: The Bornholm Museum, 1999.

Kure, Henning. "Hanging on the World Tree: Man and Cosmos in Old Norse Mythic Poetry." In *Old Norse Religion in Long-Term Perspectives: Origins, Changes and Interactions.* Edited by Anders Andrén et al. Lund: Nordic Academic Press, 2007.

Lang, James T. "Some Late Pre-Conquest Crosses in Ryedale, Yorkshire: A Reappraisal." In *Journal of the British Archaeological Association.* vol. 36 (1972): 17–19.

Leahy, Kevin, and Roger Bland. *The Staffordshire Hoard.* London: The British Museum Press, 2009.

Lindow, John. *Norse Mythology, A Guide to the Gods, Heroes, Rituals, and Beliefs.* Oxford/New York: Oxford University Press, 2001.

Looijenga, Tineke. "Texts and Contexts of the Oldest Runic Inscriptions." In *Northern World* 4. Leiden/Boston: Brill, 2003.

Mees, Bernard. "The Celts and the Origin of Runic Script." In *Studia Neophilologica* 71 (1991): 144–55. Also in opposition to pair theory: *Arkiv før nordisk filologi,* 33–82.

Milful, Inge. "Hymns to the Cross: Contexts for the Reception of *Vexilla Regis prodeunt.*" In *The Place of the Cross in Anglo-Saxon England.* Edited by Catherine Karkov, Sarah Larratt Keefer, and Karen Louise Jolly. Woodbridge, Suffolk: The Boydel Press, 2006.

Murphy, S.J., G. Ronald. "From Germanic Warrior to Christian Knight: The *Heliand* Transformation." In *Arthurian Literature and Christianity: Notes from the Twentieth Century.* Edited by Peter Meister. New York: Garland, 1999.

———. "The Light Worlds of the *Heliand.*" *Monatshefte* 89, 1 (Spring 1997): 5–17.

———. "*Mid alofatun*: secular beer, sacred ale." In *Interdigitations, Essays for Irmengard Rauch.*" Edited by Gerald F. Carr et al. New York: Peter Lang, 1999.

———. *The Owl, the Raven, and the Dove: The Religious Meaning of the Grimms' Magic Fairy Tales.* New York: Oxford University Press, 2000.

———. *The Saxon Savior: The Germanic Transformation of the Gospel in the Ninth-Century* Heliand. New York: Oxford University Press, 1989.

———. "Yggdrasil, the Cross, and the Christmas Tree." *America* 175, 19 (December 19, 1996): 16–20.

Nepper-Christensen. *The Church of St Lawrence, A Brief Description of the Round Church of Østerlars*. Translated by Stuart Goodale. Allinge, Bornholm: Gornitzkas Bogtrykkeri, 1989.

Neuner, Bernd. "Das norwegische Runengedicht – was sich hinter den Zeilen verbirgt." In *Runes and their Secrets: Studies in Runology*. Edited by Marie Stocklund et al. Copenhagen: Museum Tusculanum Press, University of Copenhagen, 2006: 233–45.

Nielsen, Anna. "Art and Architecture." In *The Cambridge History of Scandinavia*, vol. I. *Prehistory to 1520*. Edited by Knut Helle. Cambridge: The Cambridge University Press, 2003, [esp. 327 ff.].

North, Richard. *Heathen Gods in Old English Literature*. Cambridge Studies in Anglo-Saxon England 22. Cambridge: Cambridge University Press, 1997.

Novak, Sean. "Schrift auf den Goldbrakteaten der Völkerwanderungszeit." PhD diss. Göttingen: Georg-August Universität, 2003.

Ó Carrgáin, Éamonn. *Ritual and the Rood, Liturgical Images and the Old English Poems of the* Dream of the Rood *Tradition*. British Library Studies in Medieval Culture. Edited by Michelle P. Brown and Scot McKendrick. London/Toronto: The British Library and University of Toronto Press, 2005.

Odenstedt, Bengt. *On the Origin and Early History of the Runic Script, Typology and Graphic Variation in the older* Fuþark. Uppsala/Stockholm: Almquist & Wiksell International, 1990.

Old Churches of Bornholm. Edited by Ann Vibeke Knudsen, translated by Stuart Goodale. Rønne: Bornholm Museum, 1999.

Old Norse Religion in Long-term Perspectives, Origins, Changes, Interactions. (An international conference in Lund, Sweden, June 3–7, 2004.) Edited by Anders Andrén, Kristina Jennbert, and Catherina Raudvere. Lund: Nordic Academic Press, 2006.

Orton, Fred, and Ian Wood, with Clare A. Lees. *Fragments of History, Rethinking the Ruthwell and Bewcastle Monuments*. Manchester: Manchester University Press, 2007.

Page, Raymond I. *An Introduction to English Runes*, 2nd ed. Woodbridge, Suffolk/Rochester, NY: The Boydell Press, 1999.

———. *Runes*. London/Berkeley: the British Museum/University of California Press, 1987.

———. *Runes and Runic Inscriptions, Collected Essays on Anglo-Saxon and Viking Runes*. Woodbridge, Suffolk: The Boydell Press, 1995.

Parker, Elizabeth C., and Charles T. Little. *The Cloisters Cross, Its Art and Meaning*. New York: The Metropolitan Museum of Art, 1994.

Patrologia Latina. Jacques-Paul Migne. Paris: Migne, 1844–64. Reprint, Turnhout, Belgium: Brepols, 1982.

The Poetic Edda. Translated by Carolyne Larrington. Oxford and New York: Oxford University Press, 1996.

The Poetic Edda, vol. II: *Mythological Poems*. Edited with translation, introduction, and commentary by Ursula Dronke. Oxford: Clarendon Press, 1997.

Perry, Joe. *Christmas in Germany, A Cultural History*. Chapel Hill: University of North Carolina Press, 2010.

Reiher, Herbert. *Norwegische Stabkirchen*. Oslo: 1944.

Roesdahl, Else. *Viking Age Denmark*. London: British Museum Publications, Ltd., 1982.

Rohann, Michael Scott, and Allan J. Scott. *The Hammer and the Cross. Oxford: Alder Publishing*, 1980.

Runes and Their Secrets: Studies in Runology. Edited by Marie Stoklund et al. Copenhagen: Museum Tusculanum Press, University of Copenhagen, 2006.

The Ruthwell Cross, Papers from the colloquium sponsored by the Index of Christian Art, Princeton Universit, 1989. Edited by Brendan Cassidy. Princeton, NJ: Princeton University Press, 1992.

The Saga of King Hrolf Kraki. Translated with an introduction by Jesse L. Byock. London: Penguin Books, 1998.

Sawyer, Birgit.*The Viking-Age Rune-Stones, Custom and Commemoration in Early Medieval Scandinavia*. Oxford and New York: Oxford University Press, 2000.

Schwab, Ute. "Runen der Merowingerzeit als Quelle für das Weiterleben der spätantiken christlichen und nichtchristlichen Schriftmagie." In *Runeninschriften als Quellen interdisziplinärer Forschung: Abhandlungen des Vierten Internationalen Symposiums über Runen und Runeninschriften*. Berlin: Walter de Gruyter, 1998: 376–433.

Seebold, Elmar. "Das *fuþark* auf den Brakteaten-Inschriften." In *Das fuþark*. Berlin/New York: Walter de Gruyter, 2006: 157–67.

———. "Fuþark, Beith-Luis-Nion, He-Lameth, Abğad und Alphabet. Über die Systematik der Zeichenaufzählung bei Buchstaben-Schriften." In *Sprachen und Schriften des aniken Mittelmeerraums, Festschrift für Jürgen Untermann*. Edited by Frank Heidermanns et al. Innsbruck: 1993.

———. "Was haben die Germanen mit den Runen gemacht." In *German Dialects, Linguistic and Philological Investigations*. Edited by Bela Brogyanyi and thomas Krömmelbein. Amsterdam: The Benjamins Publishing Company, 1986: 525–83.

Simek, Rudolf. *Dictionary of Northern Mythology*. Translated by Angela Hall. Cambridge: D. S. Brewer, 1993. (reprinted, 2000, 2006, 2007) [*Lexikon der germanischen Mythologie*. Stuttgart: Alfred Kröner Verlag, 1984].

Simms, Douglas. "The Sun and the Saxon *Irminsûl*." In *Vox Germanica, A Festschrift in Honor of James E. Cathey*. Edited by Stephen J. Harris, Michael Moynihan, and Sherill Harbison. Tempe: University of Arizona Press, 2012.

Skeat, Walter W. "The Order of letters in the runic 'futhorc.' " *The Academy, A Weekly Review of Litterature, Science and Art*, vol. 38, no. 968 (Nov. 22, 1890). London: J. Murray, 1890, p. 477.

Stanton, Robert. Review of "Ritual and the Rood." In *Book Reviews/Religion and the Arts* 12 (2008): 602–29.

Stocker, David. "Irregularities in the Distribution of Stone Monuments." In *Cultures in Contact, Scandinavian Settlement in England in the Ninth and Tenth Centuries*. Edited by Dawn M. Hadley and Julian D. Richards. Turnhout, Belgium: Brepols, 2000.

Storsletten, Olga. *Borgund Stave Church*. Oslo: The Society for the Preservation of Ancient Monuments, 1995.

Strzygowski, Josef. *Early Church Art in Northern Europe with Special Reference to Timber Construction and Decoration*. New York: Hacker Art Books, 1980.

Sturluson, Snorri. *Edda*. Translated by Anthony Faulkes. London: Everyman, 1995.

Sundell, Michael G. *Mosaics in the Eternal City*. Tempe, Az: Arizona Center for Medieval and Renaissance Studies, 2007.

Taylor, Isaac. *Greeks and Goths*. [Oxford: E. Pickard Hall, 1879.] Breinigsville, PA: Nabu Press, 2010.

Thieme, Adelheid. "Gift Giving as a Vital Element of Salvation." In *South Atlantic Review*, vol. 63, no. 2 (Spring 1998): 108–23.

Thompson, Victoria. *Dying and Death in Later Anglo-Saxon England*. Woodbridge, Suffolk/Rochester, NY: The Boydell Press, 2004.

Thorborg, Karsten. *Aakirke (River Church) Bornholm*. Translated by H. C. Lorentzen. Rønne, Bornholm: Folkekirkens Menighedsråd, 2011.

Thurston, Herbert. "Sign of the Cross." In *The Catholic Encyclopedia*, vol. XIII. Edited by Charles G. Herbermann, et al. New York: Appleton, 1912: 785ff.

Treharne, Elaine. "Rebirth in the *Dream of the Rood*." In *The Place of the Cross in Anglo-Saxon England*. Edited by Catherine Karkov, Sarah Larratt Keefer, and Karen Louise Jolly. Rochester, NY, The Boydell Press, 2006: 145–57.

Turville-Petre, Edward Oswald Gabriel. *Myth and Religion of the North*. New York: Holt, Rinehart, Winston, 1964.

Uvdal stavkirke forteller. Nils Friis. Uvdal: Nore og Uvdal kommune, 1992.

Valebrokk, Eva, and Thomas Thiis-Evenson. *Norway's Stave Churches, Architecture, History and Legends*. Translated by Ann Clay Zwick. Oslo: Booksenteret with the Fortidsminneforeningen, 1997.

Vox Germanica, A Festschrift in Honor of James E. Cathey. Edited by Stephen J. Harris, Michael Moynihan, and Sherill Harbison. Tempe: The University of Arizona Press, 2012.

Webster, Leslie. *Anglo-Saxon Art, A New History*. London: The British Museum Press, 2012, and Ithaca, NY: Cornell University Press, 2012.

Weiser, Francis X. *The Christmas Book*. New York: Harcourt, Brace and Company, 1952.

———. *Handbook of Christian Feasts and Customs, The Year of the Lord in Liturgy and Folklore*. New York: Harcourt, Brace and Company, 1958.

Wienberg, Jens. *Bornholms Kirker i den ældere middelalter* in *Hikuin 12*. Moesgård, DK: Forlaget Hikuin, 1986.

Wilson, David. "Scandinavian Settlement in the North and West of the British Isles: An Archaeological Point-of-View." In *Transactions of the Royal Historical Society*, fifth series, vol. 26 (1976): 95–113.

———. "The Vikings' Relationship with Christianity in Northern England." In *Journal of the British Archaeological Association*, 30 (1967): 46 ff.

Zimmermann, Christiane. "Runeninschriften als Sprachakte?" In *Das Fuþark und seine einzelsprachlichen Weiterentwicklungen*. Edited by Alfred Bammesberger and Gabriele Waxenberger, et al. Berlin: Walter de Gruyter, 2006: 434–52.

INDEX

Note: Page number in italics indicate figures.